LIVE HARD

Thoughts on living fearlessly,
creating success, and embracing the future.

TODD DEWETT, PH.D.

Copyright © 2020 TVA Inc.
All rights reserved.

No part of this work may be reproduced or transmitted in any form or by any means, electronic or mechanical, including photocopying and recording, or by any information storage or retrieval system, except as may be expressly permitted by the 1976 Copyright Act or in writing from the publisher. Requests for permission should be addressed in writing to:

TVA, Inc.
1500 Hadley Street #2592
Houston, TX 77252

ISBN: 978-1-7344344-1-5
Library of Congress Control Number: 2020918975

Book editing and layout by Barbara Lindenberg, Bluebird Designs

Book cover by Chris Strain

The advice and strategies found within may not be suitable for every situation. This work is sold with the understanding that neither the author nor the publisher are held responsible for the results accrued from the advice in this book.

www.drdewett.com

DEDICATION

To those who have dreamed, worked tirelessly, failed, and tried again. To the brave people in all walks of life who push back and demand more of themselves and others. To the geeks and rebels who forge their own paths. To the friends, family members, and others who support us when we strive to be more. To the entrepreneurs who create new things and inspire. To the educators and thinkers who give us the tools. To anyone who believes that more is possible.

This is for you.

TABLE OF CONTENTS

LIVING FEARLESSLY 11

Live Hard 13

Original Fear 24

Dance Anyway 32

Sacred Cows Make Great Barbeque 43

Put Up, Or Shut Up 51

Battling Bureaucracy 63

The Comedians' Contribution 74

The Price of Deviance 83

Hell Gigs and Haters 94

CREATING SUCCESS 103

Mirror, Mirror 105

Purpose and Passion 122

Sacrifice and Perspective 137

Free Your Brain 147

Leave a Mark, Not a Stain 162

The Poet and the Meathead 171

EMBRACING THE FUTURE 181

The Truth About Diversity 183

Thank You, Ferris 196

The Gender Evolution 202

Safety, Superstar, or Rebel 210

A License to Lead 223

A CALL TO ACTION 241

INTRODUCTION

To live hard is to live fully. That might mean different things at different times. Sometimes it means throwing caution to the wind. Other times it means clinging to discipline to ensure focus and achievement. Sometimes it's about the necessity of sacrifice or having the courage to do the right thing. It's often about upending the status quo. It's always about dreaming big and living bigger.

The idea for this book began while I was a young professor and was asked to teach an elective MBA course focused on creativity, innovation, and change. I loved teaching that course. We had fun, we took risks, and people learned a lot. Some of those lessons are noted in the pages that follow.

I told the students I intended to write a book encompassing the principles we covered. Originally, it was going to be more traditional, similar to a textbook, or maybe streamlined like *The Little Black Book of Leadership*. That would be very useful, but these topics are emotional and deserve a format that allows the emotions to breath. Thus, the stories, essays, and rants you'll find here.

Many people deserve credit for these ideas. Mostly, however, I'm thankful for the kids in high school who followed their own path: the skaters, outcasts, misfits, and nerds. I was friends with a few of them. Others I admired from a distance. Most kids dreamed of joining the cliques of cool kids in school. Not me. I wanted to be a confident outsider, a punk, an honest original for better or for worse. It took me nearly thirty years to achieve that level of honesty, but I made it. So, thanks.

For me, live hard means to zealously chase meaning and success on your own terms. You have to do this in the face of too many people in your life who preach caution. This comes from love, but only serves up safety disguised as wisdom. Live hard is a paradigm that suggests it's righteous to try, fail, learn, and try again. Life is about reaching for what is possible while happily accepting the inherent challenges associated with striving.

My assumption is that if you're reading this, you want to accelerate the progress in your life. There are so many specific tools I wish to discuss, but in the end, you just need to know how to do three things: live fearlessly, create success, and embrace the future. Each of these interrelated topics receives about one third of the book. Every chapter will motivate, inspire, and add perspective to your journey. I'll also give you various targets for action – things that need to be shaken up – whether some of your behaviors or beliefs or aspects of your professional life.

Remember, this is "live hard," not "live easy." Improving your current situation will take a lot of work, and it's not risk-free. To make your team better is even harder. Improving your entire department or division, even harder. Changing your entire organization, immensely harder. Changing your community, changing the world – infinitely harder. No need to fret! It all starts with you improving yourself, one small change at a time.

Read the book. Work on you. Start to think bigger. Choose one meaningful target for change. Make progress. Repeat. Have fun!

LIVING FEARLESSLY

LIVE HARD

We need guiding ideas and beliefs in life. Sometimes we find them in very unexpected places. They guide us in ways we can't predict. In my case, I imagined a career in business: marketing, consulting, executive roles. Somehow, I instead became an educator, a writer, and a professional speaker. It only took one specific idea to change my fate.

Most days I arrived at work in my blue jeans, motorcycle boots, and a t-shirt – standard gear for my quick commute to work. Dressing however you wish was the norm at Hyperglot Software. It was a classic small startup. They created cool software that helped people learn to speak new languages. They made me employee 32, even though I was only an intern.

Jeans and a t-shirt were the norm, but when I showed up for my interview, things were a bit different. My Brooks Brothers suit, a starchy white business shirt, and a simple red tie completed my interview attire. I proudly reeked of "business student." I didn't know what to expect, though I had read about many software startups and was excited to gain first-hand knowledge.

A man opened the door of the small office building after I knocked once. He was a young man with a long goatee, a tank top, camo shorts, and no shoes. I thought I was in the wrong place.

"Can I help you?" He inquired as he looked at me with a worried face.

"I'm here for an interview," I said. I asked if I was in the right place and explained that I was there to interview with Phil, the president of the company.

A look of clear understanding washed over his face. "Oh!" He grimaced. "You're the MBA." It wasn't a question. It was just a condescending acknowledgement.

I got the job that day but not before meeting a host of Camo Short's wonderfully eccentric colleagues. I met the COO, Scott, who politely suggested that I should remove my tie and never wear one again, lest I harm all things creative. Next was the firm's lead programmer, Sam – a delightful young man who loved wearing his multi-colored beanie cap with a propeller on the top. He was followed by a fascinating Russian programmer named Nadia. She looked unapproachable, but was actually kind, with a deadpan humor that was excellent. This was a supremely colorful group.

The two main owners of the company were Phil and Martin. The former was the business guy who focused mostly on finance, accounting, and sales and marketing. He was literally the only person who ever dressed up at work. The latter was a Ph.D. in languages, a university professor, and the company's chief language and technical officer.

I was working at my desk one morning when in walked Martin, aka Dr. Rice. I'd been an employee for about one month, and at the office that day for maybe three hours. I was focused on work and beginning to think about lunch, but Dr. Rice had other plans.

"Let's go." He said. "We're going to get a tattoo." He smiled and raised his eyebrows, as if to say, "Are you in?"

He didn't actually ask if I was interested or inquire if I had plans for another tattoo. He only knew that I already had a couple, likely wanted more, and most importantly, that he was in the mood to get his next piece.

Normally, I try to be thoughtful and plan things out. This amount of spontaneity would usually frazzle me. However, I said yes without much hesitation.

It was hard to say no to this odd and congenial fellow. His intelligence and status were a beautiful mismatch with his worn jeans and sleeveless t-shirt.

Moments later, Martin hopped on his Harley. I jumped on my Honda, and off we rode, ready to play hooky. We arrived at our destination some thirty minutes later. It was a small, old tattoo shop in the hills outside of Knoxville, Tennessee. Two grizzled looking old biker types were manning the shop. Martin spoke to one, and I worked with the other.

On the fly I decided to share a fragment of an idea I had with the artist. I told him I had a motto of sorts floating around my head: the phrase, "Live Hard." I told him it was a reminder to live fully, to live in the moment, to be bold, etc. The idea was half formed to say the least, but somehow, I didn't care.

"Nice," the artist responded. "What kind of images are you thinking about?"

"Maybe a shield and a banner, or something?" I suggested.

I wasn't quite sure, so I looked at Martin. He sensed my hesitation, then spoke up. "Look man, sometimes you have to think deeply, and sometimes you just need to let go and roll with it."

"How about I put a dragon on the shield?" my grizzled artist asked.

"Do it," I replied – and then I let go. Two hours later the motto was seared onto my left upper arm, complete with shield and dragon. That day changed me.

I was already in a growth state of mind. My graduate program at the University of Tennessee was fun and challenging, and my interest in business was ever-widening. Working in such a progressive, fun environment at Hyperglot pushed me to open up even more.

My new motto was always on my mind. It sounded too silly to share with others, but I thought about it nonetheless. I wondered if others had used that phrase. I wondered if it meshed well with any teachings from religion, philosophy, the world of self-help, or elsewhere – so I started to read.

After I graduated, I did become a consultant as I had planned. I kept reading in my off hours. It became something of a hobby. The more I read, and the more I thought about it, the more I started to believe I'd stumbled upon an important phrase. I've always tried to be a person who lives by some set of principles, and though I sampled various religions and philosophies, I'd never really found what I was looking for.

Unsatisfied, I turned to one of my favorite sources of wisdom – my mother. I showed her the tattoo. She was unimpressed, but was interested in the motto and my quest. Her advice: read the Bible.

So, I did. It was my second reading. There is a great deal of wisdom in those pages. Thoughts about family, hard work, justice, kindness – you name it. There's a lot to like: the gospels are interesting, the trippy sci-fi writing is interesting, the poetic beauty of Psalms is interesting too. Of course, there is also a lot of difficult violence and mayhem, and endless amounts of begatting. It was interesting, but I still wasn't satisfied.

I dove into philosophy and psychology as well, both of which I had enjoyed as an undergraduate student. I felt energized and emboldened to learn that Vogel said discovery is the primary driver in life. Of course, I was also moved by Freud who suggested the real driver was pleasure. I was heartened to realize that Confucius, Jesus, and many others suggested that helping people was among the highest of callings.

A few of the legends in the self-help world made an impact too. The great Zig Ziglar reminded me that your attitude, not your aptitude, will determine your altitude. Campy, but the more you think about it, the more you realize it's true.

Thankfully, Wayne Dyer reminded me that you can be miserable, or you can motivate yourself. Either way, it's your choice.

I was very interested in the idea of improving myself, maxing out my potential – call it what you'd like. I had no idea I would eventually turn this interest into a career.

As I began to look for patterns or themes among all of these ideas, something obvious stood out. There was plenty of talk about things to think, say, or do in order to be good. There were rules and suggestions about things to avoid and how to stay out of trouble. That's useful, but it still felt very incomplete.

In my reading, I noticed that the ideas about becoming more, taking risks as a principled choice, chasing goals, and being successful all seemed to be missing. Face your fears. Dream. Imagine. Be creative. Embrace change. It seemed like such an obvious topical omission.

For a while, I felt like I had said something useful when I coined the phrase "live hard." Of course, as the years rolled on, I realized a couple things.

First, the world of psychology and the social sciences, and a lot of the self-help world, did indeed address these topics – at great length.

There was everything from studies of entrepreneurial personalities, discussions of fears and risks, and a vibrant stream of research around goal theory – not to mention one of my all-time favorites – Maslow's Hierarchy of Needs in the motivation literature. Sure, it turned out his theory wasn't exactly correct, but boy was it useful and popular. Many people still remember the pyramid and what's at the top: self-actualization!

Not too many years later, I was a young Management professor. I kept reading. There were many ideas about failure being great and necessary, a true catalyst for learning, a beautiful requirement for success. Scholars were studying these issues in several disciplines. Business leaders espoused many related platitudes. Self-help gurus all had their own version of these ideas. Try, grow, learn, achieve!

However, nobody had crystalized this group of related ideas in a manner that was easy to remember and share. I caught a glimpse of my arm in a mirror one day and realized that I already had the answer: live hard. By now, the tattoo was a decade old, but the idea seemed fresher than ever.

It became a part of me the day I skipped work to get some ink with Dr. Rice. Way back then it just seemed like a fun indulgence, a light-hearted idea. Years later, I realized it's so much more. It's a motto, a calling. It's a profoundly important reminder that life is short and needs to be lived to the fullest. The implied lessons also became clear.

First, question everything. This will serve you in life and in your career. Question, search, and listen. Don't be like so many alphas who sometimes talk too much – think! I don't care about which specific paradigm, religion, or system works for you. The point is that they're only worth following if there is legitimate room to question, disagree, and apply your own perspective. Any philosophy centered on ideas like try, fail, learn, and grow isn't possible without room to make it your own. The more you question the wisdom that is presented to you, the more you'll eventually find wisdom that works for you.

Second, take action. Sure, thinking and questioning are sacred, but there is something even more sacred: action. Nothing stimulates thought like trying something. When you try things you know how they feel, based on experience. On an individual level this should remind you to get off of the sideline and get into the game. Life is not a spectator sport. Try! Win or lose, succeed or fail, so what. Learn something, try again, and improve. Over time, this is always the best strategy for gaining knowledge and success.

Finally, realize that success is a journey, not a destination. The dream is to enjoy the time you spend working because you love yourself, you enjoy those with whom you work, and you see purpose in your work. If you live hard, you'll end up winning more than losing, but trying and learning and seeing progress is the real thrill. Taking your thoughts, abilities, and accomplishments forward to new levels – that's joy.

I felt emboldened by my time at Hyperglot. Dr. Rice showed me that you can be professional and still be you without a ton of compromise. We're still connected online all these years later. He's now in his 80s. Recently, he saw one of my posts on LinkedIn, a draft of what became a chapter in Live Hard about how businesses today have to get serious about embracing young talent (i.e., Thank You, Ferris). He dropped a comment and suggested to me that we better also pay attention to how older people add value. He was right again.

Isn't it interesting how change begins in your life? It's about taking one small risk, one small action. Sure, you need to think and use good judgment, but sometimes you just have to let go. That gets the ball rolling. In my case, it led to a new tattoo, a phrase on the license plate of my first Harley, and the book and story you're reading. I honestly try to live by this idea, and now I'm reminding you to do the same.

It all started with a scratchy tattoo that probably needs to be touched up. However, the truth is that no tattoo is ever as strong as the idea for which it stands.

Life is short – live hard.

ORIGINAL FEAR

Have you ever wondered what it is you're really scared of? We all have moments of hesitation, moments when we question ourselves and feel unsure. But what is it we really fear?

The usual suspects are failure, rejection, and criticism. These are secondary fears. Typically, we feel these fears when we think about doing something. Fear is a short-term response designed to keep us safe when we think about acting. On a much deeper level, our primary drive is to live: explore, try, do! To take action. It's how we're wired. Stated differently, the original fear is fear of not doing – fear of not living. This drives a desire to act and the predictable secondary fears that follow.

Too many people crumble over time when faced with these secondary concerns. They forget the original fear – that amazing reminder of why we're here. They slowly cease seriously considering interesting actions, and they make only the safest moves. Their life is safe, but unfulfilling. I think I've always known this, but it was a great speech that really brought it to life.

In my career as a professor, I used videos in class as a complement to the mix of lectures, stories, and activities I was using. I bet most of those students will always remember what Sir Ken Robinson taught us about creativity in his immensely well-received TED talk. I know it's impossible to forget the emotional speech shared by coach Jimmy Valvano at the 1993 ESPY Awards show.

One of my all-time favorites used in class was provided by Steve Jobs, the Apple co-founder. It was the famous Stanford University commencement address. He had recently, at least for a while, won his battle with cancer, and he used the speech as an opportunity to reflect on life. It was a truly a great talk about the fragility of life and the need to live fearlessly. He helped many of us shift our perspective. He reminded us to not pay attention too closely to those protective secondary fears.

His first main point was to be sure to connect the dots. Your experiences in life often reveal very useful insights, but only if we look backwards and try to connect them. After getting bored, Steve dropped out of college and chose to drop in on a few classes he liked, including a calligraphy course. Later, this heavily influenced the beautiful typography on the Mac, and, eventually, how words looked on screens throughout the world. The lessons: follow your interests, take time to reflect and look for patterns, don't live passively, and allow life to inform you.

Next, he reminded us that life is full of love and loss. Few things were as powerful as the joy he would experience as Apple thrived in the early years, except maybe the pain he felt when he was later forced out of the company he had started. You will feel highs and lows, wins and losses. This is normal and to be expected. You can't avoid the hard parts and there is no need to dwell on them. It's part of the process.

Finally, he talked about the universal nature of death and what that suggests for life. During his fight with cancer, he recalled looking in the mirror every day to ask himself, "If this were my last day, would I want to do the thing I'm going to do today?" It made him focus on adding value and chasing passion. That's a brutal but useful test we should all consider.

He was addressing what I think of as the original fear, and realized that all the rest were mostly unfounded secondary fears. There is no reason not to follow your heart, chase the dream, and seriously try to live fully. He understood that death is universal and predictable, thus not worth fearing. Instead, we should fear not really living. That's the original fear.

Not too many years later, when Jobs eventually passed, it made me think not only about his contributions, but also about the three times I too had faced death.

The first time I almost died I was in the third grade. I saved a kid named Trevor who fell through the ice on a partially frozen pond as we walked to school. We should have both died, but somehow, we didn't. The second time I was a freshman in high school. I woke up one morning in immense pain. My appendix decided it needed to explode. Thanks to one seriously fast-driving mom, it was surgically removed before real damage could be done.

The third time was quite recently. One of my clients held a big event at the Texas Motor Speedway and they asked me to deliver a keynote. They also offered me a ride in a real NASCAR race car with a professional driver. I would just be a passenger and they assured me it would be safe. I was scared and thrilled at the same time.

When the time came, I put on the big protective suit and helmet and they helped me climb through the small open window of a very mean looking machine. Five other people who were attending the event were also helped into cars lined up in front of mine. They strapped me in and off we went. It felt like we were in a rocket. It was far more frightening than fun at first.

As we hit the second turn, I remember thinking it just seemed impossible to control these monsters while turning at well over 100 miles per hour.

I was starting to feel more exhilarated than frightened. Suddenly, the car only twenty feet in front of us began to spin out. Once, twice, and then it slammed into the wall. I thought, "I hope they don't die!" Then I realized we might be in trouble too.

As smoke covered our windshield, my driver jerked the car hard to the left – an emergency maneuver that may have saved our lives. We missed ramming into the other car by about three feet. All of the cars pulled off the track as emergency personnel rushed towards the accident. The driver who crashed was fine. His civilian passenger was shaken up with a bloody gash on her chin, but was mostly okay.

I was shaking, reliving the whole thing in my mind over and over. I had a few minutes to just think. I felt lucky. I resolved never to do that again. Box checked. Thanks. I'm done.

It was right then that the lead driver walked up to our group, apologized for the mayhem, and offered to take us all out on the track one more time to finish what we started.

"Let's go," said the woman with the bloody chin. She approached the group, having been cleared by the medics. Her smile mesmerized us.
I wanted to be done, but I also wanted to finish this simple task. I didn't want to be controlled by those secondary protective fears. I wanted to

embrace the original fear. I smiled back. We all agreed to join her. It was a hell of a ride.

Slowly but surely, with the help of a few friends along the way, I've learned to use common fears as reminders of the original fear. It's a proactive way of positioning them in your mind as catalysts, not obstacles.

I've often wondered how others feel about these experiences. In particular, I've wondered many times how people who are much older think about these issues as they look back at life. With a little research, I found several studies that begin to address this question.

It turns out, when we are near the end and look back, we regret not being honest and not speaking up. We regret not lightening our load by burying the hatchet and letting go of certain things. We regret not taking chances in our careers and lives. We regret not traveling enough and not trying new things.

Stated differently, we're mad we didn't do certain things, not that we tried and did not like them or tried and somehow failed. Most of our short-term fears are just the things that stop us from conquering the one original fear – fear of not truly living.

To me, there are only two main groups of people at the end. On the one hand are people who increasingly sense their mortality. This makes them more and more conservative with their thoughts and behaviors. They fall prey to inactivity while getting lost in the predictable secondary fears. This is the bigger group of people, the one with more regrets. The only thing that scares them more than death, is life.

Then we have those who realize life is short and should be experienced fully, risks be damned. They try many things. Win or lose, they want to give things a shot. In the end, they know they did what they could and have very few serious regrets, and tons of great memories. They don't have to fear death, because they chose to fully live.

Sometimes it takes a near-death experience to really understand what it means to live. Cancer, for better or worse, is a common example. Thanks to a cancer story I've been sharing on stage for years, people share their stories with me. As a result, I met a man who lost a testicle, a woman who lost both breasts but replaced them with a rose tattoo, a salesman whose girlfriend was dying of cervical cancer, and a man in his late sixties with late stage prostate cancer who seemed more alive than nearly anyone else I'd ever met – among many others.

Of course, you don't have to have a brush with death to realize the truth. The truth is that when you're near the end, you want to feel like you truly lived. I suspect that the more we feel this is true, the easier it is for us to let go and accept what comes next.

So, actively check those secondary fears. Call them out as the imposters they are, as unworthy competitors in a contest you intend to win. You'll take some hits and experience rough waters along the way. It won't kill you. With the right perspective, it will make you stronger.

That's why I love NASCAR. Not because I care about cars or high speeds, but because what happened on that track gave me the gift of perspective. It was a moment I needed to experience in order to realize that Mr. Jobs was right when he reminded us to "stay hungry, stay foolish."

I certainly don't deny that fear plays an important role in helping us steer clear of trouble. However, they too easily derail our progress. Indulging them can too quickly becomes a habit. Remember, it's okay to have fears. The goal isn't to become fearless. It's to live fully in spite of them.

DANCE ANYWAY

Some people spend a lifetime trying to fit in. I understand. I tried for a while when I was young. What I eventually discovered is that trying to fit in prevents you from embracing the real you. Don't get me wrong, whether young or old, I understand the social benefits of fitting in. They include more friends, moments of affirmation, more status, and a feeling of being included. It makes you feel as if you matter. It does have value.

Of course, the price is heavy. Deep inside you know you're experiencing a false sense of self-worth predicated on adhering to group norms. It means you must look acceptable to them. You must speak in a manner they like. You must protect others in the group, even when you don't want to. Ongoing acceptance depends on maintaining behaviors which often run counter to your natural interests and beliefs.

Why do we feel so compelled to expend massive amounts of energy trying to be something we are not? Mostly, it's due to fear. Fear of rejection. Fear of being judged. Fear of being lonely. And, at certain ages or in certain cultures, we may even fear the experience of violence. These are very understandable concerns that can represent a heavy burden.

However, big challenges aside, I want you to stop worrying about fitting in. I'm giving you permission. No, sorry, scratch that. I don't have that right. Give yourself permission. Just be you. It's a tough choice, but ultimately, it's the only choice. Life is fleeting, so why not experience it on your terms? I often feel that people live like caged animals, trapped inside others' expectations. It's time to open the cage door and run!

Think about what you stand to gain: less wasted energy, friends you can trust, a feeling of self-acceptance that is distinctly better than any sense of acceptance derived from fitting in, a sense of honestly owning your choices, feeling more comfortable in your own skin, and a sense of personal integrity. It takes time, but these are real benefits.

The key to happiness and success isn't fitting in, it's self-leadership. That's the process between following and being ready to lead. You have to spend considerable time building meaningful self-awareness to drive personal growth and development, thus positioning yourself to lead when you feel you're ready, or when the opportunity arrives and you need to be ready.

To be clear, following isn't all bad. However, if it's chronic in the face of questionable leadership, or if you wish to lead and fail to even try, it can be a problem. Whether talking about friends in your social life or people at work, you can start the process of more fully owning your life by correctly confronting the many difficult and uncomfortable moments we all encounter. Situation by situation, one decision at a time.

There were many pivotal moments like this for me. Times when you want to go in one direction but feel somehow compelled to move in another direction. In these moments, sometimes you cave and end up embarrassing yourself. Other times you stay true to your beliefs, even if there is social risk. Two moments in particular stand out in my memory.

The first involved what were known as parachute pants. In middle school, pants that looked as if they were fabricated from parachutes were all the rage. They were shiny and had zippers everywhere. They were beautiful and I coveted them anytime someone walked past me in the hallway. I imagined how great I would look. Finally, many months after the trend faded, I scraped together all of my pennies, added a few bucks from my parents, and bought a pair on clearance. When I wore them to school, I was the only one still wearing them. People stared. I felt stupid and decided to never wear them again. Fail.

The second moment came years later. I was in my twenties and was dating a woman named Allison. We were at a Christmas party hosted by one of her friends. The music was superb. The living room in this person's house was quite large, like a dance floor, yet no one danced. Then it happened. *Bizarre Love Triangle* by New Order started playing, and I wanted to dance. Allison was off talking to friends. I was standing by myself and imagined that dancing alone would be a spectacle. "Who cares," I thought, and danced anyway.

For the first few minutes, I was alone, gyrating and moving to the best of my ability. I closed my eyes and started to let go. I could feel the sweat on my brow and I didn't care. A minute or two later, I opened my eyes and saw Allison dancing next to me. Then another friend joined, and another. Later, someone said they couldn't believe I was dancing alone. They said it was cool. I told them that was ironic since I wasn't trying to be cool. I was just trying to not care how others felt for a few moments, so I could enjoy the song.

When we were young, we all desired to fit in and be cool. Acceptance was about doing what others do. It was often about self-aggrandizing. It was sometimes about denigrating the outgroup.
Then a shift began. Sometime in the late 80s and early 90s dorks and nerds started to become cool. Some called it geek chic. It was interesting, but still

the cool kids dominated. At least the geeks created interesting subcultures, from the Dungeons and Dragons crowd (which I sometimes indulged), to the tech nerds, to the emo kids dressed in black. Later in the 90s and into the 2000s the real fun began. A far more interesting reality emerged.

Authenticity became a new form of cool. No parachute pants required. Just you. That movement has been building ever since. That's why today's youth gives me hope. They are growing the authenticity movement. It's reflected in the books they read, the movies they love, and the shows they watch. More slowly, it's happening for adults at work as well. Success requires that we embrace all colors, all genders, all shapes and sizes. And it's not just about success. It encompasses appreciation, well-being, and even love.

Being real is an all-together healthier mindset, a sure sign of human progress.

Just a few year ago something happened that reminded me of this issue. My oldest son, Paxon, had just attended his first school dance. He was in the eighth grade. The next day I was talking about it with his mother (Laura, my favorite ex-wife), and that lead to a conversation about what we remembered from school dances. We laughed as we recalled the clothes, the music, our youthful apprehensions, etc. I had the pleasure of reliving that conversation with my wife Cheryl when I got home that night. Fun memories.

The next day, Cheryl and I were at Laura's house dropping off the boys after picking them up from school. Parker asked permission and then ran in the direction of a friend's house. Paxon grabbed his basketball and headed towards the park in the lot next to their house. I needed to chat with Laura when she got home from work, so Cheryl and I took a stroll in the neighborhood to kill time.

An hour later we stood by the short metal fence outlining the park watching Pax shoot hoops. Laura pulled up on her bicycle, small radio affixed to the handlebars blaring 80s tunes. She was wrapping up a quick after work ride. When she arrived, *Tainted Love* by Soft Cell was playing. I knew from a text exchange that she was about to tell Paxon to come home for dinner. She waved him over.

"I love that song," I said. "It reminds me of a club we used to go to in college in Memphis."

Cheryl chimed in, "Remember $.25 cent beer nights?"

"I remember $1 beer nights. How old are you?"

She did not like my remark and socked me hard on the arm.

Paxon walked up and rolled his eyes when he heard the music. He was fourteen years old. What did he know? He thought that Drake was the only thing that mattered that year.

"I was so broke," Laura said. "I think it was ladies' night that got me and my friends through college."

Paxon quickly tired of the music, and our conversation. "Yell at me when you're ready," he said as he slipped back towards the basketball court.

"Stay here. We're leaving in just a second," his mother said.

Just then, *Girls Just Want to Have Fun* by Cyndi Lauper started playing on Laura's speaker. We adults all started bobbing our heads with the song.

Pax looked perturbed and seemed to become aware of the presence of other people around us. Several adults were walking near us. Several more kids of different ages were playing in the park. Once again, he started to slowly step away from us, basketball in one hand, his own Bluetooth

speaker in the other. He was praying that no one he knew would see him standing with us.

Cheryl pulled out her sarcastic voice, "Where do you think you're going?"

We all knew two things. One, he hated "our" music. Two, he wanted to keep playing basketball.

"Fine!" Pax said in an unpleasant tone. He pressed a button on his speaker and another on his phone. Drake's song *Controlla* began playing at a high volume.

I took a few rapid steps and grabbed the speaker playfully out of his hand and turned it off. Using his fourteen year old lingo, I said, "That's not fire. That's garbage."

I was trying to be funny, but he looked offended. Cheryl and Laura were happy – Cyndi Lauper was once again clearly audible.

"That's not cool," Pax replied. Again, the tone was a bit too full of teenage angst.

"Be nice kid," I said.

He smiled a tiny bit, then asked in a low voice, "Or what?"

"Or we'll dance, smartass!" I yelled.

"Y'all old people don't need to be dancing," my son had the guts to say.

Laura's speaker went silent for just a moment as the song ended. Willing to do battle with her son, she immediately turned up the volume on her speaker not knowing which song might play. That's when we heard the unmistakable introductory riff of *Jessie's Girl* by Rick Springfield. When Rick started saying, "Jessie is a friend...." I decided it was time for action.

I looked at Cheryl and nodded. She looked at Laura, raised her eyebrows and nodded. The three of us broke out in dance. It was awesome! Three out-of-shape middle aged white people shaking it like we had a clue. We did not, nor did we care.

There was a split second when Pax heard *Jessie's Girl* that he looked as if he'd be okay, no doubt capable of enduring yet another 80s song. Then we started shaking and gyrating.

I know I must have looked like a chubby Herman Munster in athletic shorts. The ladies seemed to be doing a really bad imitation of the famous Molly Ringwald dance from The Breakfast Club.

Pax froze in pure shock and embarrassment.

One lady jogging by us smiled and pumped her fist in support of our antics.

Pax's face honestly looked like he had just walked in on his grandparents having sex. He began power walking away from us towards home, ready for dinner – ready for anything other than these three crazy adults.

We finally came to our senses, high-fived and laughed. It's not always the case that parents get to feel cool and in control with teens, but we certainly won the battle that day.

Sometimes being authentic and just doing your thing draws in people who like what you're up to. Other times, it repels them. Either way you win: you don't have to pander or beg or fake it at all. You just have to let people know where you stand.

I was texting with Pax later that night. He said the only way you can ruin a good song was to let us dance to it. However, he also said he thought we had guts. That's pretty cool.

Even though there is a normal age-based divide between me and my teenage son, I take pride knowing that, while imperfect, he's not one of the obsessed clique members at school that I so clearly recall from my time in middle school and high school. His Drake-fueled attitude aside, he's one of the laid back kids, very solidly a part of the love-everyone authenticity movement. That makes me happy.

I'm not naïve. I know that today we still have a version of the clique system at school and at work, but the cliques no longer wield the power they once did. In fact, there is now sometimes a cost associated with trying too hard to fit in. We call those people fake or trendy or plastic. Even considering the never-ending trolls online, on average, we're making progress and trying to embrace a higher-level interpersonal ideal.

I'm also not suggesting that to be yourself you should shun all social norms or strive to be different just for the sake of being different. Nor am I suggesting we act in a manner that intentionally embarrasses others. I just think that it's good that we're seeing a shift away from traditional strict notions of "fitting in" and "cool." Inclusion is becoming much more than a good idea. Groups and cliques will always exist, but they're becoming kinder, slowly but surely.

So, what about you? Where are you in terms of authenticity?

My advice: don't worry about them. Do you. Start now, because it gets easier with time. To those of you leading the way – young or old – thanks and congratulations. To everyone else, give it a try: dance anyway. Sometimes they will love it. Other times they might run from you. Most of the time, I think you will find that when you march to beat of your own drummer, others usually want to join the band. If they don't, at least you'll enjoy the music.

SACRED COWS MAKE GREAT BARBEQUE

Innovation can happen when a select few individuals in an organization step up and try new things. However, it's much more likely to have impact and be sustainable when everyone believes in the organization's innovation culture. Over time, a culture that is serious about change is always stronger than one or two innovators.

One of the most enduring hallmarks of any effective innovation culture is the ability to deal with sacred cows. This refers to a custom, behavior, product, process, or rule that is known to all as unproductive and yet untouchable. Much respect to my Hindu friends and their reverence for cows, but the phrase is now so much bigger. It's a general reference to something that is above criticism – something that can't be touched, but should be.

Simply stated, most sacred cows are not sacred! They are simply choices that became long-standing routines. These routines become accepted as the way we do things, and, endorsed by enough people, they eventually become untouchable.

The concept is used most often at a macro level, addressing rules, processes, business models, and markets. The examples are plentiful. No one ever thought Microsoft Windows was the best we could do, but it has been accepted historically as the operating system standard by the majority of computer users and developers on the planet. Then Linux was created. Then computing went mobile, and Android sprung to life. Sacred cows don't last forever.

Consider cars. The internal combustion engine has been mostly obsolete for decades. Yet it has persisted very successfully. Similarly, the dealer network approach to sales has long persisted. This was the only buyer reality until recently. Tesla chose to upend two sacred cows, deciding to sell fully electric cars directly to consumers. They are now the most valuable car company in history.

Nothing lasts forever. Things are supposed to change, in business as in life. The more interesting issue is whether or not you benefit from change, or more to the point, whether or not you're helping to create the change. Do you over-indulge the routine, or slay the cow?

Let's take it down a level and focus on your workplace. Think about that executive perk that is unjustifiable. The fact that we're always expected to work weekends. That crazy dress code.

The vacation policy you loathe. The terrible system of accountability at work that allows low performers to always get by. Sound familiar? There are a million examples.

The same happens in your personal life. There are things that exist, that you respect and don't question, that are supposed to help you or guide you. Maybe they once did, but they don't any longer. It could be an old friend, a personal belief, or possibly a practice or a habit. Whatever it is, it stops you from growing, being more productive, and being happier. You're starting to realize that change is needed. Is it time to question one of your sacred cows?

Let's make some barbeque. What you target is up to you, but let's be honest, we all have multiple targets. It might have to do with your religious beliefs. It could have to do with your diet. Maybe it's your family traditions. How about the pronouns you prefer? Who knows? You can't hold on to any standard or tradition just because you always have.

Don't worry, I'm not telling you to upend everything you do! We only have a certain capacity for personal change. Target one or two things that matter to you, and make the decision to be brave. Choose to no longer step over the dead body in the room as if it were not there. Good news, gaining comfort with making change slowly increases your capacity to make more change. With persistence, change might eventually become transformation.

Sure, it can be risky. Yes, it takes guts. Sometimes it might even be painful and cause problems between you and others in your life. It's your choice. You can play it safe by not rocking the boat, or you can roll the dice and attempt real change. I can promise you this much – great things are more likely to happen in your life when you address a few sacred cows. The possible fallout is worth it.

The benefits are undeniable. You stand a chance to change and improve the thing in question (the behavior, the policy, the belief, etc.). You elevate your level of consciousness, reducing the likelihood of future sacred cows becoming a problem, show others what you stand for and how strong you are, and you learn how to communicate about the need for change more effectively.

One of my favorite examples ever involved a former MBA student in a course I was teaching dedicated to creativity and innovation. One of the themes in the course was inspired by the Einstein quote, "We cannot solve our problems with the same thinking we used when we created them."

There is plenty of research in various areas of business and psychology that supports this idea. The practical application in the course was to encourage the students to go find new perspectives for the biggest problems they face at work. I specifically asked them to target a sacred cow and start making barbeque. I remember at least two students who voiced loudly that they thought this sounded fluffy, and wondered about the importance of the assignment.

Near the end of the term, everyone shared what they had learned from the assignment. One student who took the task seriously worked for a manufacturer of various pieces of equipment used in underwater applications. His company professed a strong belief in innovation, but one of their sacred cows was that you were not supposed to discuss your problems outside of your division. Each division chased similar top line metrics and to partner or share with other divisions was tantamount to helping the competition.

Thankfully, this student, an engineer by training, really liked barbeque.

He targeted a particular material that was prominent in several major products sold by his division. The goal was to find something cheaper and hopefully stronger, and it had to conduct electricity effectively under enormous underwater pressure. Even though people openly questioned what he was doing, he spent time in three other divisions and even had meetings with two key suppliers. Eyebrows were raised.

He eventually found the new material he needed; a particular alloy he didn't even know existed. It was cheaper. It was stronger. It had all the qualities he was looking for. The costs savings were projected to be in the millions in the first year alone, not to mention the new revenues that were likely due to the fact that the material made the product more attractive in the market.

The student's boss, one of the company's senior engineers, initially questioned him, but decided to stay out of his way. In the end, he was so pleased that he sent me a very kind email encouraging me to continue my practical teaching methods. With the student's permission, I read the email to the class. As people clapped and high-fived him, I refrained from directly staring at the two students who so brazenly questioned the assignment weeks earlier. With any interesting endeavor, there are always doubters.

Or maybe you'll feel inspired by one the most famous sacred cow stories ever told – it's the story of Dick Fosbury. As a high school high jumper in the 1960s, Dick used the acceptable jumping method, called the straddle method.

It was the only acceptable method at the time. You go over the bar face down – first your torso, then one leg, then the other. Unfortunately, Dick just couldn't master the technique.

However, he was curious and began to experiment. Quickly one of his efforts started to dominate his attempts. He tried to jump over the bar face up, with his back facing the bar. Initially, he had a little success, but nothing major. It just looked bizarre to most observers, one of whom suggested he looked like he was having an airborne seizure. His coach was not initially supportive.

When he started, he couldn't complete jumps at five feet high with the standard technique. With the new technique, he began to make significant progress. They made fun of him, but he continued making progress. A local reporter derided his method and called it the Fosbury Flop. Dick was not deterred and continued to improve.

Soon enough, he set the school record for his high school. People started to take him seriously. Dick eventually won multiple NCAA championships, and Olympic Gold in 1968 in Mexico City by jumping over seven feet, three inches. Today, nearly all competitors around the world use the Fosbury Flop method.

Innovation isn't always beloved when it's first proposed or first attempted. Most people cringe when someone attacks a sacred cow. So what. Persevere. They'll come around. If they don't, try again. Light the match and start the fire.

Or, you can join the chorus of voices claiming that there is no need for change, that's already been tried, or saying that it won't work. Those are all defeatist mottos. Instead, choose change. Don't ignore the dead body in the room, even if you're the only one who sees it.

To achieve a dream and find real success almost always requires some form of innovation. Innovation, in turn, almost always requires you to deal with a sacred cow or two – whether making personal change or leading an organization.

What are you waiting for? Start cooking. I want to smell some barbeque.

PUT UP OR SHUT UP

Organizations have long promoted their list of values and beliefs. These are espoused values. They go by many names: core beliefs, values, mottos, etc. What's more interesting, of course, is the extent to which these are merely espoused values versus enacted behaviors.

You've all seen these lists of ideas: honesty, integrity, innovation, empowerment, community, courage, accountability, love, etc. The list is endless. In fact, it seems quite impressive, doesn't it? Unfortunately, we all know that sometimes the list reflects the behaviors we see, and sometimes it does not.

It's time to call bullshit. Get real or go home. The more classic refrain is "put up or shut up."

To determine where your organization stands, begin by examining the congruence between what you say and what you do on a regular basis. As a firm, are you consistently walking the talk, or are you just attempting meaningless public relations? The former builds immensely valuable trust.

The latter is a problem, and if you do it consistently you can cause real damage.

Let's think about what it means to say that your group is lacking congruence between espoused and enacted values. There are several levels of bull between stating your values and living your values.

Level one is about neglect. You have a list of some sort that you can find on the website, but in truth, you and the team haven't talked about it for years. The list is old and you don't know if you're actually aligned with the ideas on the list or not. In essence, you really don't have a list. At this level, problems are likely in the near term as people with whom you do business realize the obvious – you're full of bull.

At the next level, you have a good list but you're not really living it. You say your employees are your biggest asset, but you're happy to downsize while throwing big paydays at top executives. You say you love the environment, yet your firm is spewing out unnecessary pollution. Eventually, the incongruence catches up to you. It impacts your ability to attract and retain talent, and it impacts how customers feel about you.

Then we have the level to which you really must aspire. Here, you have a thoughtfully prepared and maintained list of values, and, mostly, your behaviors look like they were clearly informed by these values. This is a special place where the value you add to others (e.g., employees, customers, vendors, partners, the community) feels amplified. Showing congruence in this manner is a form of group or organizational integrity. It builds confidence, and makes you shine in the eyes of most observers.

However, even more is possible. Once you personally learn to embrace congruence and transparency, the conversation should spill over into your larger business ecosystem. For example, for world-class firms, it's natural to make joint decisions with partners that are openly influenced by shared values that matter. I firmly believe this idea should apply to us as individuals as well.

So, what level currently defines you?

I know from experience that many of us struggle with this topic. One piece of evidence is a values-related activity I've used for many years at certain live events. I ask people if they know what they really value most in life. Often indignantly, people say, "Yes!" Then I ask them to write down their top five values. Then I ask them to rank them. Eyes roll, headaches begin – the words don't easily flow. Point made. Too often there is a gap between what we espouse and what we can articulate – let alone what our behaviors say.

Here's the rub – even if you know what you really value, you still have to figure out what to do when you have to interact with others who may not share your values. It's inevitable. We all face this struggle.

In my life, a great example concerns how I run my business. On occasion, I am asked to speak under conditions I can't accept. Sometimes this involves how I look while on stage for a client. Several times over the years I have had to turn down lucrative deals in order to be congruent with my values. My brand aligns my beliefs, the messages I share, and how I look and speak. So, when a client asks me to wear a suit and tie, I have to say no. Sorry AIG. Sorry ULINE. I believe in authenticity and honesty, so, no – I don't wear suits or ties.

That's just a tiny, easy to handle example. Many times, the situation is much more difficult. My favorite example that demonstrates this involves a story a man shared with me after a live event in San Diego. When I left the stage, he quickly made his way to me and introduced himself. His name was Noah.

"Have I got a story for you," he said.

"I'd love to hear it," I replied.

Noah told me where he lived (a small town near San Jose, California) and that he was his town's newest and youngest city council member.

"The age issue is significant since the group is dominated by baby boomers, with no millennials like me." He continued, "After I started it was just a few months of really boring meetings, until something exciting finally came up. It was a plan to revitalize our little downtown area."

"That is exciting," I said.

"I thought so too, at first," he replied. "The members leading the effort began by suggesting a few items we could all support – things like repairing sidewalks, installing a needed traffic light, and tearing down two old condemned buildings."

I could sense that he was about to drop a bomb on me.

"However," Noah said, "At some point, they mentioned an item that surprised me. They suggested we needed to find a way to close the tattoo shop in the middle of downtown, or force them to move out of downtown."

Like all members of my audience, he knew I was fond of ink. So I said, "Let me guess. You're a tattoo person? Got a few tattoos?"

"At the time, no." He continued, "But I was intrigued and asked why we would need to close or move the shop. One person, our senior member by age and tenure, spoke up and declared in a matter-of-fact tone that the shop attracts the wrong people and represents a barrier to improving downtown."

He continued, "Not one person spoke up to challenge him. I wanted to, but I knew that there would be months of discussions and work before any big decisions could be made. Frankly, reading the faces of the other members, I didn't think he would get the support he needed to actually go through with it. I was a little confused too since I'd never been in the shop and wasn't sure how to feel about his comments. He just sounded, well, too judgmental. It made me think about what it is that we stand for. Our values."

"What did you do?" I asked.

"I just waited and kept going to our regular meetings. Sure enough, he made sure to keep that item front and center in our plans. No one said a word in opposition. Finally, one night another member finally asked him why he felt this made sense. What he said bothered me. He told the group the shop was attracting the wrong kind of people. He specifically referred to them as 'bad clientele.' Since he and the other members were all gray haired sixty-somethings, I think I knew what he meant – but I had to ask anyway."

Noah said that when a break finally came up in the conversation, he decided to speak up. He asked his colleague, "I was wondering – can you help me understand what the problem is with the shop's clientele?"

Silence engulfed their small meeting room. Everyone stopped what they were doing, turned to the senior member, and waited.

"Well," his colleague began, "I just think it's clear the business attracts the wrong type of people for our downtown."

"Okay, what type of people do you feel they attract?" Noah asked.

The senior member was annoyed. "Look," he said, "Tattoo shops attract people who want tattoos. I don't think that is the crowd we want to invite downtown."

Noah refused to let go. "What is it about people with tattoos that represents such a problem?"

Another member jumped in and changed the topic. Surprised, Noah decided to let it go for the moment. He sat quietly, feeling uncomfortable and unsatisfied.

Later that night, when the meeting was over, he headed straight downtown to the tattoo parlor. Sacred Heart Tattoos was a small shop in the middle of the main strip downtown. He simply planned to sit in his car and observe who was coming and going. An hour later, Noah had witnessed nearly twenty people enter the shop. He noticed nothing meaningfully different about these people compared to all of the other people entering nearby eateries and shops.

He decided to investigate further, got out, locked his car, and walked into the tattoo shop. At twenty-eight years of age, Noah had not been in a tattoo parlor for nearly a decade, and had never himself been inked.

Once inside, he heard that sound so familiar to those of us who enjoy the art – the buzzing of the tattoo machines. Two customers were getting work done. An additional two people he believed were employees were walking around.

One greeted him. "Hi, can I help you?" she said. He introduced himself, learned her name, and noted that she was heavily tattooed. When she learned he was on the city council and just stopping in to say hello, she decided to sell the shop a little.

"Oh. Well, welcome. We're in our eleventh year now. The shop strictly complies with all state of California rules for safety and health. We employ a team of ten, either full-time or part-time, and eight of us actually live here in town."

She said as she reached for a tablet, "we've been pretty successful the last few years." As she spoke, she flipped through a series of pictures on the tablet showing members of the team, various award-winning tattoos, trophies, and press articles. She locked eyes and plainly asked, "Are you sure you don't want anything?"

Noah surprised himself. He laughed out loud, pulled out his wallet, and threw down two hundred dollars. "Give me something nice," he said.

She laughed and then opened the gate separating the lobby from the main shop, allowing him to walk into that sacred area.

The following week Noah arrived at the city council meeting reinvigorated, ready.

Necessary yet boring municipal items packed the first hour.

He sat restlessly and wondered if he would have the guts to do it. He didn't want to lose his spot on the city council. On the other hand, he didn't want to be part of a group willing to so easily dismiss a harmless and productive group of people.

Finally, his senior colleague spoke up. "Can we address our options now for the Sacred Heart shop?" he said. "I think we can all agree the fastest way to make this happen is through zoning changes."

The group sat quietly. A few looked at Noah, seemingly encouraging him to say something now or let it go forever.

"Wait!" Noah said. "Before we talk about options, we still haven't addressed why we're talking about them in the first place. I'm not comfortable with this for a few different reasons. First, I think this means of expressing yourself is normal these days. It's mainstream. Second, I visited the shop and met the staff. They're nice people. I mean…"

Noah was interrupted by the loud voice of his senior colleague. "Maybe they are nice, but people looking for tattoos? Is that our target market?"

"So, they're just 'bad clientele'?" Noah replied.

"Not all of them, but many – yes!" the older man stated. "They are more likely to be deviant, uneducated, and inappropriate. There – I said it." He sat back in his chair and glared at Noah, as if to say, "Top that!"

Noah stood. They all assumed he was leaving in protest. Instead, he began unbuttoning his shirt. Moments later, standing there in his t-shirt, he showed the group his new tribal tattoo on the upper part of his left arm. "I graduated from UCLA. I've started two successful businesses and managed two others. I'm happily married. I'm a father. I'm on the city council. Do you want me to avoid going downtown?"

After a few silent moments passed, Noah said that others finally spoke up and agreed with him. The issue was tabled – permanently.

I grinned as he finished telling me the story and then lifted the sleeve of his golf shirt to show me his tattoo. It was a simple piece that felt anything but, after hearing the story.

Noah, now in his forties, grinned back at me. "I'm happy to report that Sacred Heart Tattoos has just celebrated their thirtieth year in business – and our little downtown is doing quite well," he added.

It was truly a joy watching him light up as he shared his story.

Sometimes it's hard to live your values and do the right thing. It doesn't always mean that things will work out, but it does always mean you will feel a little better and sleep a bit more soundly.

I definitely believe in the power of organizations to move us forward on issues that matter. However, I believe in individuals like you even more. Maybe stating what matters at the top of our organizations and hoping these values will flow down the hierarchy isn't the best way to make change. Maybe it starts with you and me. Maybe the organization moves forward when a few key people – whatever their role might be – choose to do the right thing.

Maybe it's time for us to put up or shut up like Noah.

BATTLING BUREAUCRACY

We've all made fun of bureaucracy, right? Bureaucracy is an organizational reality that involves a hierarchy of authority with a defined reporting structure, rigid division of labor and control of resources, and lots of formal and informal policies and procedures for everything. People fill assigned roles and work on goals that help the organization function.

It's pretty easy to make fun of bureaucracy. I've done it many times privately in conversation, in writing, and on stage. We've all had the experience of dealing with wimpy bureaucrats: they don't have a spine and never take risks, they love rules and pay too much attention to politics, and they don't care about progress as much as adherence to process!

That probably sounds worse than it actually is, which is one reason bureaucracy has so few fans. Many executives, thought leaders, and pundits refer to it as a villain, a cancer. Others call it evil, a disease, evidence of poor leadership, and any other derogatory thing you can think of.

I penned a few popular quotes over the years that try to capture these sentiments.

"And when the Devil saw them making progress, he grinned and invented committees."

Everyone can relate to that one. Committees, of course, evoke thoughts of the most hated manifestation of bureaucracy: meetings! Which leads to another quote.

"In poorly run meetings, time moves at the speed of stupid."

These are somewhat true, and definitely funny. Nonetheless, I believe it's important that we rethink this idea just a little. I loathe simple black and white thinking, which is rarely as useful as it sounds. To suggest that bureaucracy and red tape are simplistically evil is wrong. A more nuanced understanding is needed.

Look at it this way: bureaucracy is necessary and useful, can sometimes be very problematic, and definitely requires a few brave people to keep it in check.

First, yes – bureaucracy is a necessary evil. It is required to gain some amount of control over complex systems. The benefits are very clear and very important. They provide centralized power in times of need, give clarity about how to act in a given situation, serve as a hedge against hasty or poor decision-making, provide rules for resource use, and much more.

However, we all know bureaucracy can stand in the way of progress. The simple solution to this challenge is a small, consistent supply of brave employees willing and able to grapple with the worst manifestations of bureaucracy.

This refers to people willing to speak up, disagree, and advocate for change. More to the point, it includes those willing to take risks on behalf of needed change, and especially those willing to fill leadership roles. But change often begins with just one or two brave souls.

One of the more famous examples of mavericks successfully bucking the system involves Pacific Tech's Graphing Calculator software. They helped people visualize numbers and data like never before. The story of how the product's two developers were able to sneak it into shipments of Apple's PowerPC computers is the stuff of legends.

Ron Avitzur was a contractor at Apple whose project was cancelled. He decided to un-cancel his small part of the project that involved the graphing calculator. Apple failed to take his badge, so he just kept showing up at work.

Some people knew he was working on a cancelled project. They loved the product and admired his renegade spirit. Slowly, as he shifted from one temporary unauthorized workspace to another, real employees began to offer help.

Early on, Ron recruited his friend Greg, another non-employee. The pair used every form of subterfuge possible in order to keep pouring hours into this officially cancelled product. They quickly became underground heroes at Apple. Software geeks, technicians, and several managers pitched in to keep development moving forward.

Things were running smoothly, until they got busted and kicked off campus.

They immediately began sneaking back into the office to continue working in whatever unused space they could find. People were impressed, and many people continued volunteering their time to help – even though they might get in trouble.

Of course, this was all fun and games unless the product could be seen by customers. Thankfully, the lead engineer responsible for all software loaded onto all PowerPC computers was a fan. He told them he would break the rules, risk his job, and include their program on the machines to be shipped.

When executives discovered what they were up to, they loved the product so much, they decided to support it – officially. The next thing you know, the program was properly tested and localized in many different languages. They no longer had to hide, and eventually, they even received vendor badges so they could enter the building legally.

The bureaucracy tried to stop them in different ways on several occasions. Thankfully, it failed.

The product was shipped in 1994. Students and teachers around the world loved it. The graphing calculator helped millions grapple effectively with math. They were hackers, driven by joy and a fair amount of luck, who did whatever it took to get the job done – for free, at great personal risk. (For those who might be interested, here is the original full story: https://www.pacifict.com/Story.)

The Graphing Calculator story feels a little like a beautiful fairytale. It has a sweet ending and nobody got hurt. Most stories about fighting bureaucracy aren't so pretty. Reputations can be harmed. Jobs can be lost. Careers can be derailed.

However, before you make big moves that might kill your career, you merely have to make one choice. When confronted with a bit of absurdity, what do you do? Let the bureaucracy continue to win and decrease your capacity for innovation? Or, speak up and try to enact change, or at least a needed conversation?

I've had the opportunity to ignite conversation many times for my clients. My role as an outsider often allows me to say things that insiders can't say. The issue is clear, people should talk about it, but – thanks to fear of failure, fear of evaluation, fear of excess work, fear of damaged reputations, etc. – nobody speaks up. Except me.

I was once hired to speak to the management team of one major division of a large medical device manufacturer. I was given one hour to offer some sort of leadership wisdom and entertainment. Before I was due on stage, I was sitting in a nearby room with an employee who'd been assigned to stay with me and make sure I got to the stage at the right time.

She was an HR manager for the division. Her name was Alice and she seemed like a terribly nice person. We enjoyed chatting while killing a few minutes before the show. At one point, I asked what she and her team were up to lately. She smiled and began telling me about their efforts to help innovation by streamlining and improving the HR policy book.

"So you're looking for red tape to cut?" I asked.

"Yes. Just looking for things that are unnecessary or too ambiguous to be useful," Alice replied. "We spent a lot of time last week working specifically on grooming and attire."

I was intrigued. A red flag sprang up violently in my head. "Really?" I said, trying to act normal.

"Believe it or not," she continued, "we spent the better part of two days just trying to decide the rules for ladies' footwear in the office."

"What was the issue?" I inquired, while suppressing my laughter. I now understood that they felt they were helping the company, but in reality, they were creating more red tape.

"It's all about open toe versus close toe shoes," Alice continued. "As it tuns out, it was harder than we imagined agreeing on definitions for what was or was not acceptable. It started with a woman who basically wore sandals to work. Her boss brought it to us to inquire about any relevant policies, and we thought the existing rules were really fuzzy, so we tried to fix them."

They had violated one of my top leadership rules: never create a system level response to an isolated local issue. Instead, the local manager fixes the issue and moves on. Otherwise you get bloated policy books really fast.

"So how'd that go?" I asked.

"Well, three hours into our debate about women's shoes, we realized we were going to need to take some pictures," she said.

"Pictures?" I replied.

"Actually, we ended up getting all of the pictures we needed from the internet. Instead of trying to define exactly what was or was not acceptable, we just gathered different images of shoes we felt were generally acceptable versus those that were not. The whole thing took most of the day."

I was about to respond when the door opened.

"You're on in five minutes Dr. Dewett," the person said.

"Okay, thanks," I replied.

Alice smiled and directed me out the door, down a hall, and into the back of a large auditorium. They quickly attached my microphone. An executive delivered a flowery introduction, and I walked on stage.

You never really know what kind of crowd you're dealing with until you're out there. This was a great crowd – ready and willing to think, smile, and laugh a little. I was cruising through a few of my signature stories, people were taking notes, nodding, giggling – it was a good gig.

At some point I felt a little distracted. I found myself deviating from my script. I don't actually have a memorized script, but I do tend to stay on topic. I realized I was adding a few more comments and anecdotes than normal, and I finally realized why.

I was talking about leadership, specifically aspects of leader behavior and how they relate to creativity and innovation. My subconscious was kicking me in the proverbial shins, compelling me to get real and just say what was on my mind. A fairly seasoned risk taker, I decided to just be honest.

In the middle of a story that was being received very well, I stopped, paused, and just looked at the audience for a moment.

"Let me ask you a question," I said. "Did you know that this company has an odd fixation on ladies' footwear?"

The audience was shocked and puzzled. A few people instinctively laughed at the absurd nature of my comment. I explained what I had learned from Alice (I did not name her or mention her group), and then launched into a talk about what it means to focus on things that really matter.

Near the end of my impromptu rant, I noticed Alice, now standing in the back of the auditorium. The expression on her face suggested that she wasn't terribly happy with me. The talk went really well, even if I did adlib a bit too much. Importantly, the point was made. The client got it. They seemed to appreciate my content and candor, which turned into additional speaking opportunities. I never heard from Alice, and I hope she didn't get in trouble.

The issue that caused this situation is a very serious one indeed. We have a finite amount of time, energy, and resources at work. It's vital that we use them to address things that are essential and things that can really move us forward. If we mismanage our time, we should err on overinvesting in things that really matter.

It turns out that bureaucracy is like a drug. When you allow too much time to be wasted on rules, policies, committees, and meetings, you get used to it. You build a tolerance. This red tape approach to life becomes your norm. It becomes your expectation. It becomes a drug you need to get by. It becomes time spent arguing about women's shoes.

After the shoe incident, I began sharing versions of this story with other clients. What I found was a little surprising. I knew that by sharing the story, others would tell me stories from their organizations about bureaucracy. What I did not see coming was that the very same shoe dilemma plagues many organizations! Five additional client audiences so far have shared highly similar, and hilarious, stories.

So, if the shoe calamity is so common, imagine all of the other examples of time spent on somewhat trivial matters. There are many examples. The only real question is whether or not you'll step up and do something about it. Can you imagine what you and the team would be capable of if you were to focus only on things that really move the needle?

If you actually care about high performance and innovation, you do need a few folks willing and able to speak up. Someone has to call bullshit, and it needs to be reasonably safe to do so.

Think big here. Innovation is more than just defining certain goals, looking for waste, and launching a new product or service. It's about hiring the right people and developing them correctly. Sure, you need smart people who mostly fit in, but you also need a few people with the guts to not fit in. Otherwise, do you really believe in innovation?

Is that person you? It's okay if it's not, but if you truly want to keep bureaucracy in check, you need to find a few of these folks, hire them, protect them, and listen to them. Otherwise, you might miss out on a few game-changing graphic calculators while wasting time talking about shoes.

THE COMEDIANS' CONTRIBUTION

People sometimes tell me I seem to know a lot. It's usually a compliment, but not always. I tell them, "I've learned what I know from the classics."

They reply with something like, "You mean Shakespeare, or maybe Socrates?"

"No," I say. "Comedy classics. The great writers and philosophers are amazing, but the bravest thinkers are usually comics." Though often considered a "low" art, it is without a doubt an art.

Sure, comics can be taboo, off color, or downright profane, but much of what they say speaks to core issues in life, often with great insight – even if you don't like how they say it or it makes you uncomfortable.

I think that's why comics are so beloved. They embrace one of life's most potent truths: that growth is often uncomfortable because it requires us to face what we usually ignore. Underneath the specific issue they might be addressing, this is the ever-present lesson.

They entertain us, but even more, they push us, question us, and often educate us. Their contribution to society is immense, and often undervalued.

The great Eddie Murphy said, "If you're an artist like a really, really long time, it stops being a performance. I'm not performing anymore. I reveal myself to the audience. I show you some of me." This speaks to the vulnerability, honesty, and self-awareness that defines great comedy. People think that because jokes are crafted, they are somehow an "act." Very often, they are not just risky comments about topics, but risky comments about the authors themselves.

The best comics provide commentary to make you think without even addressing topics directly. Kathleen Madigan said, "I always give homeless people money, and my friends yell at me, 'He's only going to buy more alcohol and cigarettes.' And I'm thinking, 'Oh, like I wasn't?'" Using only a few words, she's told us to be humble, not to judge, to be kind and helpful, and that we are all flawed. Tell me that's not genius.

Possibly the bravest of all-time was Lenny Bruce. He once said, "The 'what should be' never did exist, but people keep trying to live up to it. There is no 'what should be,' there is only what is." He demanded a focus on reality, and more than any other, he was willing to get in trouble in order to be able to share his views. His combination of bravery and insight laid the groundwork for all the greats who followed.

Sometimes, comics simply elevate the obvious to remind us that we can't take things for granted. For example, consider my favorite living comic, Dave Chappelle. He once said, "The hardest thing to do is to be true to yourself, especially while everybody is watching." Of course, many others have shared similar words. None, however, have lived them as openly as Dave. No matter his level of popularity, he refuses to conform. Love it or not, you will know his honest thoughts – and they will usually make you laugh.

It's a rare mental space comics occupy. They have to understand how others think without caring too much about pleasing them. Or, as stated perfectly by Sarah Silverman, "I don't set out to offend or shock, but I also don't do anything to avoid it." It's an interesting statement about freedom. To speak and not care, or not even think about what others might say or do – that's a level of freedom few ever attain. It's also a reminder that mental and verbal freedom are not risk free.

To get away with all of this biting honesty, comics often feel compelled to move past mere candor towards critical self-analysis and self-depreciation. Maybe the best ever in this regard was Richard

Pryor, who once said, "I had to stop drinkin, cuz I got tired of waking up in my car driving ninety." His characters vividly reflected his difficult reality. His jokes were drowning in depictions of his imperfections. The self-therapy he showed us on stage became therapy for us all.

There are too many important voices to mention. However, like most of you, I have only one all-time favorite: George Carlin. For me, he's the greatest comic who ever lived. It's not because he was brave enough to fully evolve in front of us over the years. It's not because he mastered so many elements of the trade: characters, voices, observations, word play, and so on. His comedy was the greatest because it was insightful and explored issues that matter.

His work was far more intelligent than it ever was lewd or hilarious. He was a social analyst, a philosopher, and a happy nonconformist. As a nonconformist, nothing was off limits for George. Nothing! His thoughts on golf, religion, parenting, sex, flatulence, and so many other topics were visceral and enduring.

He also wasn't simple, or simply left or right. He made fun of everyone, every group – period. He also loved everyone, at least occasionally. He'd make you think about the nature of perception by saying, "Have you ever noticed that anybody driving slower than you is an idiot, and anyone going faster than you is a maniac?" He might follow this with a scathing bit about the Catholic church. Then, he might close a show, as he did many times, by saying, "Be good to yourself, and each other." Never simple, always touching.

Possibly his greatest bit ever was "the seven words you can never say on television." The point is simple and profound. I would summarize it by suggesting that we often make arbitrary rules using indefensible logic while acting like it's justified, if not righteous. Some estimates suggest there are over 400,000 words in the English language, yet as George tells us, there are only seven you can't say on television.

I'm reminded of so many similar realities in life and at work. At home growing up, most of us faced prescribed bedtimes. Is there truly something magical about 9:00pm as opposed to 8:30pm or 9:30pm? It is true that kids resent rules because all kids think they are smart enough to govern themselves, they want to be adults, and they resent not having power? I know this was true for me. We need rules.

Some childhood rules make complete sense. For example, "Don't answer the door when Mom is in the shower." However, many others are quite arbitrary and far less important. Rules about where to put dirty clothing, which behaviors do or do not require permission before engaging, and rules about running in the house are all a little suspect.

At work we see more of the same. Rules in many organizations become a disease, eating away at vitality and potential. We have rules for acceptable attire. Rules for the amount and type of personal items one might display on one's desk. Rules about under which conditions and in what amounts we can accept certain acts of kindness from vendors. Rules for which holidays we acknowledge and which we do not. Rules for when it is or is not okay to use a computer for non-work matters. The list is immense, well-intentioned, and generally questionable.

Of course, all of these rules tend to have merit. Most were created in response to a real need. Kids do need a bedtime. Employees do need guidance and structure. However, you can't act like the rules are somehow perfect and never to be violated. With a few exceptions, rules are just guidelines, solid first references. Generally, they should be respected. They give order, hedge against waste, and provide predictability in behaviors and outcomes.

However, rules don't always fit the situation and should be challenged. Carlin knew this. He marveled at the amazing array of words in the English language and rightly felt that it was absurd to call out only a few. Over 400,000 words, and yet only a few special ones were identified as not fit for television? Apparently, if you wish to break the rules and reveal yourself as deviant, you merely need to squeeze in one of these words while on television: shit, piss, fuck, cunt, cocksucker, motherfucker, and tits. At least that's how he saw it. If you'd like to hear a musical version of this punchline, I recommend searching online for Blink 182's rendition.

As I think about living fully, whether that's through honesty in relationships or creativity and innovation at work, I think about his lessons. The words you can't say on television remind us that most taboos are not really taboo. They are but arbitrary lines drawn in the sand, put there to convince us that we are good and all is right in the world. Of course, anything but is true, and George loved to point it out.

Consider his funny take on the nature of the "stuff" we all collect in life. It's about the absurdity of how much we have, how it defines us, and how it possibly restricts us. On this topic, George is more spot-on than the best of preachers. We have a problem with stuff. We give it value over other things in a manner that might actually lower our quality of life.

In the bit, it becomes increasingly difficult for the person to identify a smaller and smaller amount of his stuff to take with him from place to place. Each instance is a painful threat to a positive self-identify. The piece implies that too often we value stuff more than kindness, hard work, and integrity (among other possible traits and behaviors we might mention). It also implies that collecting stuff is more important than collecting great experiences. The very absence of any mention of these facts makes the bit work. Their absence is in fact deafening.

And who can forget his take on the Ten Commandments? In truth, there is a lot of bull and redundancy in the commandments. George concludes that two commandments very succinctly and honestly cover everything. To paraphrase: 1) Thou shalt always be honest and faithful, especially to the provider of thy nookie, and 2) Thou shalt try real hard not to kill anyone, unless, of course, they pray to a different invisible man than the one you pray to.

These two provide the perfect example of rules that allow for needed wiggle room. There is a need, a rule is thus warranted, but it's not absolute, right? Rules are just a place we should start thinking, that's all. Seriously, if creativity and innovation are ever to become more than mere catch phrases where you work, you'd better adopt this view of rules fast.

Possibly another way to reframe the ideas discussed by George, and the amazing comic community, is to suggest that questioning is the most fundamental human skill. It's a skill, it's a human need, it's a requirement for progress. It's also hard to do, threatening, and uncomfortable. Helping us through such a process while making us laugh – that's a true gift. Stand-up comedians deserve a sincere thank you, and our continued support.

In the end, the so-called philosophers may have been geniuses, but what good is genius if some core idea can't be translated and shared with the masses? Comics have long served as essential translators. They provide a much needed reality check. Their genius is practical insight, honesty, clever use of words, and bravery. They have allowed us to laugh, and to be more honest about things – especially ourselves. For this, we owe them everything.

THE PRICE OF DEVIANCE

Every organization extolls the virtue of creativity as a core asset and aspiration. It is universally beloved, or at least that's what they say.

They say that it's a beautiful higher level form of human intelligence. It is definitive proof of our standing at the top of the food chain.

They say creativity is the secret ingredient that allows high performance teams to stand out. Better teams rely on creativity to overcome any issues with talent or resources.

They say it's the essential ingredient for career success. Being a subject matter expert is no longer enough. Now, you need to be a conjurer of new possibilities.

Organizations seem to fall all over themselves begging for the stuff. Organizations of all stripes plaster the word 'creativity' all over everything: their website, the mission statement, advertising, their list of core values, etc. Creativity, innovation, change, improvement – the words used sometimes vary, but they make it quite clear that these ideas are at the heart of who they are.

There is only one problem with all of this. They are all full of hot air. They hate creativity. It's all rhetoric with very little reality.

Here's what they don't tell you.

Creativity implies risk. To suggest a new idea, to propose or enact a process change, to fiddle with new technologies, or to suggest anything other than the status quo is to suggest a lot. In your mind, or possibly the eyes of others, you're asking for time we don't have, money we don't have, and risks we don't need.

So, managers who encounter creativity rarely celebrate. They don't immediately feel good about it and seek to compliment the person or group responsible. They don't applaud, cheer, or otherwise immediately validate your efforts.

Instead, they flinch. Sometimes they react very negatively. They feel scared as they begin to envision how this thing you did or suggested will upend the current order. They see you taking risks. They see you creating work for the team. They see you doing something that hasn't been done. For all of these reasons, they feel threatened.

In short, you just did something deviant. You thought it was a good idea. Your intentions were pure. In the eyes of many others, however, you're simply deviant. Isn't creativity awesome?

The reaction doesn't matter. Be deviant. Pay the price – it's worth it.

To be an effective leader, you need to understand this truth and work towards building comfort in the face of this reality. Then your job becomes helping others do the same. You have to take the journey with them and help them rethink the risk.

I've personally bumped up against this challenge many times. Can you relate?

I recall a time early in my speaking career when I used a small rubber duck for promotional purposes. It was a red devil duck with cute horns that gave it a naughty and funny quality. Everyone loved it, until one executive at a certain large company received one, along with a note from me, and responded with a long, angry email. Based on this person's religion, it was offensive and dangerous.

There are many eyes on you. Sometimes you think you're being creative, but others might think you're simply deviant.

My father and I were quite close for many years before he passed. There was, however, a period of time where I could do nothing right in his eyes. In one month's time, I turned down a full ride to college because I no longer wanted to play basketball, started to grow my hair out, pierced my ears, and began getting tattoos. He didn't speak to me for many weeks.

Even if your track record is great and you're making progress on your goals, others won't always see it that way. Sometimes to them it just looks like you've lost your mind.

Have you ever walked into a restaurant and wondered if you were underdressed? I have. I arrived at a nice restaurant one day on my motorcycle, wearing dirty boots, old jeans, and sleeveless t-shirt. I was surprised they let me in, and everything seemed to be going okay... until President George HW Bush sat at the table next to me (he was closely associated with Texas A&M University, where I was in graduate school at the time). The Secret Service team stared at me passionately the entire time as if I were a real threat. It was a horribly uncomfortable lunch.

You think you're just being expressive and comfortable. Others think you're inappropriate and pose a risk.

More than once I've been nearly pulled off stage mid-speech. Each time was because I was telling a story beloved by nearly everyone (emphasis on nearly). It's a story about a lesson my father taught me during his battle with cancer. It's emotional, and on a few occasions someone in the audience loses it who happens to be in the middle of their own cancer-related struggle. Once, that person actually stood up and fled the room, a few other times the person just sat quietly and cried. In any case, the client was angry.

You never know the immense situational variance you face. You offer up something you feel is useful and creative, but to the ears of one or more listeners, it's toxic and unbearable. You're deviant.

I know how difficult this unexpected reality is when it hits people in the face. That's why as a professor, I took great care trying to explain it to my MBA students. However, I think we all know that it's not enough to simply hear an idea. You need to actively engage it to fully understand and appreciate it. One night in class this became particularly clear.

Class began that night just like any other. I entered the room, greeted the students, and began informally chatting and coaching. While doing that,

I started unpacking the materials in the large box I brought with me.

The students slowly started to grin as the contents of the box became clear. I neatly arranged many small bottles of bubble solution on the desk at the front of the classroom.

"Tonight you will learn a difficult truth about creativity," I said. "We'll begin the class with an activity. I'm going to give you a few instructions, then you'll grab your materials (I pointed to the bubbles) and get to work. I want each of you to grab a bottle of bubbles and leave this classroom. There isn't any need to talk. I just want you to roam the halls of the business school and find other people who are not in this class. When you find them, blow some bubbles at them. Not right on them, just near them. Pay attention to how you feel and how they act. If you're really feeling frisky, feel free to open the door of some other classroom, walk in, share a few bubbles, and then walk out."

The students looked at me like I was crazy. I was used to this.

"Any questions?" I asked. They said nothing.

Thankfully, one bold student stood up, grabbed some bubbles, and out the door he went. A few others immediately followed, and then everyone else slowly joined in.

I watched them as they strolled through the building. Most of the students were scared and did not blow bubbles until a few brave students went first. Only then did the others join the fun.

Their very tense demeanor quickly faded. As a group, they felt emboldened. The strangers with whom they were sharing bubbles looked confused and intrigued. Some laughed. Some seemed bothered, if not angry. Most just froze and seemed puzzled.

Finally, two of my students decided to enter another professor's classroom. They followed the instructions I had given. They did not knock or speak, they just entered, said nothing, blew some bubbles, and quickly left.

At the designated time, they all reassembled in my classroom. They nervously sat down. I didn't have to kickstart the debrief – they just spoke up.

"I'm pretty sure people thought we were nuts," one woman suggested.

"I had one person tell me to go away," another student shared.

"Did you guys see the janitor?" one asked.

"What?" I said.

"Yea. He'd just finished cleaning a big section of the tile floor and then we all walked through and started making a bubble mess," another offered.

They all laughed uncomfortably.

"When you did what you did, how did you feel?" I asked.

They admitted to feeling scared, nervous, and apprehensive about what might happen.

"Did you all just jump in immediately and begin blowing bubbles when you left the class?" I inquired.

"I just stood around at first," a man said. Others concurred.

"Did you eventually start blowing bubbles?" I followed up.

"Yes," they said.

"When?" I asked.

One student replied, "When I saw that others were doing it. Then I figured there's strength in numbers."

More laughter.

I gave a few brief comments about how creativity is risky, how the rhetoric is so much different than the reality, how leaders and change agents can make it okay to engage when they lead the way, etc.

"Is blowing bubbles truly a deviant act?" I asked. "Of course not, but when you do something without permission, something unexpected, something not yet tried – in the eyes of others it's likely to be deviant. In fact, it can get you in trouble."

"Dr. Dewett?" One student raised her hand as she called my name. "I just want you to know that I think we may have really upset the professor in the classroom next door." The students gasped. "Me and Stephen opened her door and stepped in. We were in there for like five, maybe ten seconds. Just long enough to dunk the wand in the bottle and blow some bubbles. Then we left."

I knew the person teaching in the next classroom. She was an economics professor – a very serious economics professor. "How did the she react?" I asked.

"The students were great," she said. "They thought it was funny. I think they knew we were from your class. The professor quickly raised her voice and told us to leave. As we turned to leave, she kept telling us to get out and to stop disturbing her classroom."

"I repeat – is blowing bubbles so bad?" I asked. "I think we can all agree that generally, no, it's a harmless act. However, to that janitor, a few other students you encountered, and to my colleague next door, your actions were deviant. Can you imagine how much stronger and more pronounced the reactions are at work when someone is crazy enough and brave enough to try and be creative? The responses can be enormous."

The next morning I received a long email from my colleague in the Department of Economics. She was very angry at the "stunt" I pulled the night before. She copied my department chair. According to her, I was callous and disrespectful. I had succeeded in ruining the learning environment in her classroom for the evening. She insisted that I had no idea how to teach and that she would continue this conversation with the Dean of the business school.

The next night in class I read the entire note to my students. They had a visceral reaction. Some laughed. A few were aghast. Regardless, they just got the point.

Creativity is beautiful just as the pundits exclaim. It's magical. It defines great careers. It's essential for the long-term success of any organization. However, even small acts of creativity can be viewed as acts of deviance depending on who's watching.

Fine! What's the alternative? To play it safe and accomplish far less? No thanks. A rubber duck, a story about your dad, your attire, bubbles, nearly anything – you never know exactly how people will react. So what? Let them pull you from the stage. It's worth it as long as you said something of substance.

To be clear, I'm not trying to create radicals. That's not my goal. But when I look out across all of the professionals I've met, the thousands and thousands I've either spoken to, coached, or observed, the reality is that most people err on playing it painfully safe. Thus, my job is to remind them that real progress requires creativity. This means that, occasionally, you have to be an intelligent deviant.

Good news: risk is something you can get better at understanding and embracing over time. When you gain more comfort and insight into engaging risk intelligently, over time you start to look clever in the eyes of others, not deviant.

Start running up that learning curve now before it's too late. Go ahead, pay the price – it's worth it.

HELL GIGS AND HATERS

For the truly successful, life is not easy. It's not all people throwing roses at you. In fact, it's often the opposite. The more successful you are, the more people will come after you in one way or the other. Sports, school, at work – it's that way everywhere. I'm not sure what that says about humans, but it's true.

It's funny how successful people sometimes like to manage how they are perceived in the face of this reality. They brag about what they have done (or allege they have done), they disavow evidence of mistakes, they blame and frame to ensure issues are understood according to their preferred narrative.

The achievers who last and leave a strong legacy don't bother with that. They know that we're all human and they try to let their actions speak for themselves. We all have bad days. They know this and don't lose focus on their amazing average simply because of a few exceptions. These exceptions are hell gigs – times that things did not work out as planned. You prepared, planned, clocked the hours, showed up ready, and should have won

– but you didn't. Things just didn't work. Mistakes were made. It seems like everything that could go wrong did go wrong. Hell gigs happen to the best of us.

Similarly, we all have haters. Call them haters, trolls, critics, or just plain jerks. Haters don't get you. They don't like you. What they do like is telling you they don't get you and don't like you. They have always existed, but today, haters are more prevalent than ever before. There are so many things with which they might find fault. They have access to your social media comments, your online comments, transcripts of meetings or online chats, texts, and a million other things they might decide to criticize. They are simple creatures to say the least, but they do remind us of something useful. No person is ever universally loved. Not Jesus, Muhammad, or Buddha – so why would you expect to be loved by all?

I've had a few good moments over the years. I'm grateful to say I have a few fans and followers. I could brag about the big named clients, the huge stages, the publications, my success as an online educator, special events like TEDx, and plenty of other things. My batting average is superb, even world class – but it's far from perfect. The truth is that I've had plenty of hell gigs and haters just like everyone else.

I once famously stood on stage in front of many leaders from State Farm and completely sucked. It was a nightmare performance from a version of me that wasn't ready for the big stage. Thankfully it became a catalyst for change and a story in a book I wrote called Show Your Ink. The State Farm story has since helped many people learn to embrace their mistakes. However, it started as a horrible day that made me want to quit speaking professionally before I'd ever really begun.

Then there was the time I showed up for a speech for a large group of international executives who spoke little English. The organizers who hired me had never hired a pro before. They did not include me on the agendas which were provided to attendees as they arrived. I was not introduced. I did not have a designated place to stand. I was just thrown in front of the group in the middle of dinner and told to begin speaking. During my speech, a little over half of the room stopped talking to listen to me. The rest continued enjoying their table conversations. More than a few people must have thought I was drunk. When I was done, they just seemed annoyed and most did not applaud. Awkward.

At another event, for the first time ever, I was nearly pulled off stage mid-speech. They turned on the lights and the event planner motioned for me to wrap it up quickly. For a moment, I thought

I had lost track of time and run long. I proceeded to wrap up swiftly. Moments later, the same planner ran to the stage to tell me it was okay and to continue for another twenty minutes. I was confused and didn't know what was happening. I heard the normal laughs while I was speaking, but due to the lights, I could not see the audience.

Apparently, a key client executive who was in the audience was triggered by one of my stories. It's a beloved story about my father's battle with cancer and what it taught him as well as me. It intentionally evokes emotions. I've told that story over one thousand times and people love it. That day, there was one exception. The client was dealing with a loved one who was sick with cancer, lost control of her emotions, began crying heavily at her table, and had to be helped out of the room. The organization's CEO, I later learned, was so angry with me that he told the meeting planner to pull the plug on my speech, leading to the odd interaction I noted earlier. What a strange moment.

Here's a good one. Take it from me, never give a speech at a Brazilian steak house. At first, I was excited. It was a talk for a group of meeting planners, but it was a lunch event – not good. There were many guys in fancy uniforms who looked like bull fighters carrying around huge sticks of meat and sharp swords for cutting the meat. The entire time I was speaking they moved around the room, clanging swords, carving meat, and presenting the single biggest distraction I've ever faced. It was worse than the few times the power went out. It was worse than the several times fire alarms had gone off. Worse still, every planner in the room felt bad for me and remembered me for all the wrong reasons.

If you hold yourself up as an expert of any kind, beware – there will be haters. I'm no exception. As a professor back in the day, most of my students loved me. I won every teaching award you can win at my university, multiple times. A few however, loathed me. A very small number of students felt that being casual, informal, light-hearted, and occasionally funny was not appropriate in a graduate education setting. Oh well. They were basically good people, but based on personality and learning preferences, they did not like me.

No person exemplified this reality more than a student I'll call Betty. Betty was in her mid-seventies. Her comments in class were disruptive, off-point, and confusing to everyone. When I stopped calling on her, she was incensed, and started speaking up without raising her hand. One night after class, the Chair of my department stopped by to tell me a student had lodged a complaint against me with the Dean of the college. It was Betty. Her allegation: I was biased against older students, women, and Asians (she was not Asian; this part baffles me to this day). She also reported that I had a caffeine addiction that needed attention. I'm not making this up. An investigation was required. Students were interviewed. I was easily cleared, but was also very embarrassed, and I had to endure the fact that she was still sitting in my classroom.

Some years later I was very fortunate to begin working with the team at Lynda.com, or LinkedIn Learning as they are now known. We were a match made in heaven. Within a few short years, we had created many courses eventually enjoyed by many millions of professionals in several different languages. Suddenly, I was one of the poster boys for successful online courses.

Every day, I receive a large pile of notes from users on that platform. The vast majority are kind and thankful. They say hello, express appreciation for particular bits of advice I've offered, tell me stories about how the content has helped them get through difficult situations, etc. That is massively gratifying. However, for every fifty fans, there is one person who hates me. Last year, something I said in a course trigged a man in Poland to call me a "Marxist sympathizer." He wrote nine paragraphs of unkind words online for all to see. He angrily questioned my credentials and threatened to complain to LinkedIn if I did not explain myself. Hey, you can't win them all.

Don't even get me started on the negativity you see on the other social media platforms. The point is that no matter who you are, you'll see hate, just as you'll see love. So, what do you do in the face of this reality? Here are five surefire ways to make sure the hell gigs don't hurt you and the haters don't win.

1. *Realize it's normal.* Choose to accept that some people will not enjoy you, will not support you, and will not encourage you. You will not be everyone's cup of tea. Not everyone loves chocolate, or the Beatles, or sports, or you – so what! Remember, you're just shooting for a great average, not perfection – as that is impossible. Michael Jordan and LeBron have haters. Lady Gaga and Ariana Grande have haters. Oprah and Ellen have haters. Obama and Trump have haters. All of them have failed more than they succeeded. They did their best and sometimes came up short. It happened to them and it will happen to you. Just accept it.

2. *Don't react.* Or, let me be specific, don't react unproductively. To the extent that it's reasonably possible, don't feed the haters and don't rage when you fail. First, haters love your sadness and anger. For a hater, that just confirms you're the weak frail person they hoped you were. When failure strikes, cry or scream for just a moment, sure, then put on your big boy

pants, take a deep breath, look in the camera and smile. Be proud that you tried. Be happy you're still standing and will have another shot. Be grateful for the chance to get it right next time. Those are the reactions that matter.

3. *Appreciate imperfections and errors.* Haters love to point out flaws. In my case, for example, they love to point out that I speak too fast. I always have. It's annoying, but true – a product of nerves, I suppose. So what? I've ironed out a million other ticks over the years, yet this one remains. Say what you'd like, haters, I have a ridiculously high average, and yes, I speak quickly. In terms of hell gigs or project failures of any kind, just remember that your errors are the superstar learning guides for your next success. Don't ignore them! Talk about them, analyze them, solve the problem they represent if at all possible, and be sure to keep them somehow on display so you never forget them.

4. *Choose to improve.* Learning is a choice. You may or may not love the haters and the failures that lay the groundwork for success, but they all represent forms of feedback. You need feedback to improve and grow. You should be happy you have something clear with which to grapple as you work to move forward. Some haters might clue you in to an aspect of your

performance you should examine. At least consider the possibility. Some hell gigs will teach you how to do things differently moving forward. That's a blessing.

5. *Finally, don't play it safe.* What's worse than hell gigs and haters initiating difficult learning? No hell gigs or haters – ever. That is a huge indicator that you're too tame, too risk averse, and too damn safe and boring. Nothing interesting has ever been accomplished without plenty of mistakes and learning moments along the way, so stop trying to avoid them. Instead, start pushing it. How will you know that you're pushing it enough? You start to mess up and a few people begin to criticize you.

You're not chasing perfection. You're chasing improvement. Along the way you will never fully please yourself, avoid haters, or steer clear of setbacks and screw ups. Good. The faster you accept this reality, the sooner these people and moments become catalysts for growth.

It's true for you. It's true for your team. It's true for your kids, family, and friends. It's true for all of us. These difficult bits of feedback push us forward and prevent us from becoming lazy.

Long live the hell gigs and haters.

CREATING SUCCESS

MIRROR, MIRROR

Self-improvement isn't difficult to understand. You just have to ask the right questions and seek answers honestly. You must be genuinely open to feedback – a terribly useful and sometimes painful catalyst for change. Feedback comes from many sources: self-reflection, observation, task performance, comments from others, opportunities won or lost, etc.

Some feedback, say a promotion or moment of praise, is joyous and easy to accept. However, many times, feedback is more difficult or ambiguous. Be careful. Simple positive affirmations feel good, but don't always help you move forward. It's the difficult bits of feedback that usually contain the insights required to move forward.

That's where your journey begins: embracing one of the most challenging sources of feedback you'll ever encounter: yourself. It's time to learn how to look in the mirror.

You have to look deeply – without flinching, without looking away, without distorting, without making excuses, and without shattering it by throwing it to the ground. I need you to acknowledge that growth often requires pain. Accept this and wear it like a badge of honor. Ready?

Let me help you test whether or not you're ready. I want you to know how comfortable you are with the real you. Here is a simple test. The next time you're with a friend, colleague, or loved one, give them your phone. Do this quickly. Don't overthink it – just do it. Give them the phone and instruct them to take a picture of you, head to toe. Tell them to do it right where you're standing. Just one picture. No more, no less.

Now tell them to post it immediately to all of their social channels with no filters, no editing, and with whatever caption they'd care to add, and to be sure to tag you. You're not allowed to look at it. It's theirs, not yours, and it's to be shared with the world immediately. For the next twenty-four hours, you are not allowed to look at the picture, or who likes it, or who comments, etc.

If you find it easy to do this, you're ahead of most people. That suggests you have a lot of self-confidence, very little worry about what others think, or both. Looking in the mirror might be a bit easier for you. Not necessarily easy, but easier.

If doing this was difficult, but you did it – congratulations. This is your wake-up call. It's time to start caring a bit less about posturing to maximize how you look in the eyes of others. You need to know that looking in the mirror will feel a lot like you feel while taking that test: worried, shaken, unsure. Accept it. This is required before real growth can begin.

If you could not do it, that is fairly normal, and, well, you have a lot of work to do. In fact, you may be lost. You are focused on things that basically don't matter, and you allow them to distract you. It's imperative that you face this issue now, before you become stuck on a journey bereft of meaning.

The point is simple, but powerful. We get lost acting, managing impressions, and resisting or avoiding real feedback. Instead of life-enriching soul searching, we passionately cling to identities that don't accurately reflect who we are. Who we really are fades into the background, shamed into silence. Social media is fun, but it's not the feedback you're looking for. What you need is a good mirror.

When you look into the mirror, you can't lie. It's the opposite of online forums and many face-to-face conversations. No posturing, just real data. You see something closer to the truth about yourself. Or, I should say, that opportunity is there, if you engage the task sincerely.

Don't prepare to look inward – just do it. When you look in the mirror and see your refection, don't perpetuate any fictions by seeing only what you want to see: your best side, best angles, the right lighting, hair just right, etc. Just see what there is to see. Expect that you'll love some of what you see and feel uncomfortable with other things you see.

Then smile, because what you're learning to value is the real you. When you gain a bit of comfort just gazing at the unfiltered you, your heart is more open and your intentions more honest. Only then are you ready to start asking useful questions that can lead to understanding and growth. What follows are the questions that guided me. Maybe you will find them useful.

Who am I and where do I come from?

Like many teenagers, I felt like I did not fit in with my family. I suppose that's just part of the universal experience of being young, pumped full of hormones, etc. My family was odd. For example, there was my brother, the outcast. He seemed to enjoy that role most of the time. We got along well about half of the time. There were a few epic fights too. Mostly, we just left each other alone.

My parents were another story. It's nearly impossible to escape your parents when you're young. They were good people, a touch simple, and often drunk.

They coped with life through libations. Mom was a sloppy, yet happy drunk. Dad was not pleasant at all most of the time. Life with them, especially my father, could be a nightmare of yelling, throwing things, and sadness. Thankfully, other than the night my dad tried to kill our cat with a shotgun, the worse thing I saw was a little shoving and a fair amount of neglect.

Then a miracle happened. Late my senior year in high school my dad went to rehab and quit drinking. The man who emerged was kind, fun, and grateful to be alive. Mom cut way back on her consumption. They were both different in a very pleasant way. I stopped hating my life and began to get to know them for the first time.

Soon enough, Dad and I began taking walks together. We talked about everything, happily solving no problems at all but enjoying the conversation immensely. One night while out walking our dog, I asked my new friend what he knew about the origins of our family.

"Well," he muttered. "I don't know for sure, but I did ask your grandfather once. He told me that to the best of his knowledge, the Dewett's sprang up from a penal colony in Georgia."

"Wait. Isn't that like a prison or something?" I asked.

He nodded.

"Like in colonial times? Are you serious?"

Dad laughed. "Yep. Clearly, we've evolved. I mean, we're not criminals now, are we?"

Through research I learned that there were many penal colonies in the early America. They were full of riff raff, or people accused of being riff raff, who were sentenced to hard labor in the new world. Many modern American families began as prisoners or indentured servants sent here from England.

Years later, when the technology allowed, I sent away my saliva to find out more of the answer. The lab worked its magic and weeks later I received the results in the mail. I am almost exclusively of western European decent. The biggest chunk is Irish (18%). I'm an Irish-infused European with precisely one percent "Jewish" DNA thrown in for good measure.

Of course, what I eventually realized is that when you really look in the mirror, your genetic history matters quite little beyond a few physical realities. What I decided is that regardless of where I got my abilities and dispositions, life is all about what I do with them. Who am I? I am what I choose to be.

It was a tentative conclusion, but I was excited when the thought hit my brain.

Who am I trying to please?

This is a question that burdens nearly all of us. How much do we owe others, especially family and friends? How much does it matter that we meet the expectations of others instead of worrying first about our own expectations?

There was a period of time during high school when I broke from the pack, began doing what I wanted to do, and stopped caring what others thought. I think it was created by the changes Mom and Dad made with regard to booze, but I can't be sure. What I do know is that I started dressing a little different, listening to new music, and dating someone very unexpected.

Her name was Lori. She was beautiful, tall, skinny, and awkward with a punk rock demeanor. When we started seeing each other, the response from the mainstream kids was swift. They made comments to me. They stared. They began to shun me with those brutal gestures in the hallway: the rolling eyes, the averted looks, the whispers. I was a well-known and somewhat popular kid, so there was a price to pay for dating an outsider.

I tried to explain all of this to Lori at one point, which prompted her to say something that helped change my life.

"It's weird to think about any of them talking about me," she said. "But I'm not sure it matters." She saw the look of concern on my face. "Wait. You really care about what they think, don't you?" she asked.

"I guess I've just never had to think about it before, you know?" I replied.

"Yea, well what they think doesn't really matter. The only thing that matters is what you think," she said.

I looked at her funky makeup, out-there hair, and awesome thrift store clothes. I knew she was right. I just knew it. I did not yet know, however, if I had the guts to live that ideal. I don't think I understood it for years, but the seed she planted grew.

Not too many months later, I began to make the first big decisions that many young people make: where to go to college, what to study, etc. The plan had been quite clear – choose one of the two schools offering me athletic scholarships, go play basketball, and study medicine or law. At least that was the plan until that seed started to grow. It quickly shifted everything in my mind.

I turned down the scholarships. My dad wouldn't speak to me for weeks. I got my ears pierced. I attended the local university. I grew my hair long, got my first tattoo, and discovered the beauty of wearing black. Dad thought I had lost my mind. I had not. I had simply chosen to answer the question.

I had decided that I must please myself in order to be happy. I don't mean to sound arrogant or self-indulgent. I simply needed to explore, be me, and chase goals that I found intrinsically appealing. As I started the journey, I did hope that I would eventually make Dad proud, but I simply refused to make that my overriding goal. It's worked out well so far. Thanks, Lori.

What do I want to be?

It was in college that my intellectual side really woke up. With no basketball to distract me, I was able to fully embrace how much I enjoyed learning. With few exceptions, I loved my classes. It was a strange and exhilarating transition. I had gone from a high school career defined mostly by not caring deeply about any classes, to a college career where I quickly found myself in love with nearly everything. I'm not sure I ever loved math courses, but everything else struck a chord: the sciences, literature, writing, history, philosophy – you name it.

After the second year, it was time to choose a major. I dreaded the choice. Typically, I'm a decisive person, but not for this decision. I could easily envision a career in so many fields. It was like my brain had recently been turned on and it delighted in all the possibilities. Soon, that positive feeling turned into fear and paralysis. I didn't feel good about saying no to so many potential paths.

That's when I met Dr. Patterson. I needed a mentor, a sounding board. I had a possible interest in a business school major, so I stopped by unplanned one day at the Dean's office looking for advice. I learned later that normally a lower level member of the staff would have seen me, but that day Dean Patterson was free. The man truly loved his students and wanted to be helpful. I was sent right in to see him.

"I think I might want to be a business major, but I don't know which area to choose. It all sounds like it would fit me. I don't know. I think I'm weird. I just like to learn, you know?" I said. I remember feeling bashful, exposed. I had not yet learned to be comfortable talking about learning or careers.

"Yes, I do know. That's why I made a career out of school. You've come to the right place," he said.

He was a kind, older man, with that grandfather quality we all love. He was a good listener and very helpful. In the end, he was one of the main reasons I ended up majoring in a business field. It's powerful what happens when we feel accepted and appreciated.

I handed him my transcripts. "I've really enjoyed my courses so far. I've been thinking about finance and marketing mostly, but I think marketing sounds more interesting."

He glanced at the transcripts, then back at me. "Todd, it sounds like you've already made your decision. You should strongly consider marketing. You find it interesting, that means you'll be a motivated student. Looking at these grades, you're going to do well no matter which focus you choose. Let me tell you about our honors program."

I eventually graduated as a marketing major with honors, finished an MBA at a different university, worked for well-known global firms, and earned a PhD. I've built a successful career in business focused on helping others and I'm loving the journey so far. Thanks, Dean Patterson.

However, just because you have the balls to ask the question doesn't always mean you'll know the answer, or like the answer, or that the answer will stick. Step one is to ask the question. What do I want to be? Then the goal is to accumulate experiences – try stuff! Keep your eyes open, listen to others, ask questions. You'll eventually make progress and find a stronger fit between what you need, what you're good at, and the opportunities that are available.

In the end, I found my calling. My first calling, anyway. It was in the ivory tower. I later found a second calling in writing, speaking, and making online courses. These things fit me like a glove. The 'try things' mantra pushes you closer and closer to the center of the black hole until you're simply pulled in and the calling reveals itself. You can't see it now, not until you allow the black hole to suck you in.

What am I afraid of?

Sorry, but I have more bad news. If you work your butt off, get a little lucky, and find your calling, that doesn't mean you'll have the guts to chase it. You'll face a seemingly unending number of constraints that will push you to resist accepting this blessing. To be clear, finding your calling is a blessing. Nonetheless, your brain will work against you and tell you it won't work.

It starts with self-doubt. Sure, you've determined that you want to be an engineer, an artist, a scientist, or a small business owner – great! But then you ask yourself if you have what it takes. You question your intelligence, work ethic, priorities, personality – all of you.

Of course you have what it takes. Even if you didn't, how could you live with yourself having not endeavored to find out? You can recover from trying and failing, but the burden of living with "what if?" might kill you.

Next, you'll wonder what others will think, especially your parents and closest friends. Will they support me? Will the judge me? Beats me, and probably. More importantly, should that stop you? You're looking a unicorn in the eye and you're worried about how others might feel about your fascination? Stop thinking, put down the camera and stop trying to take a selfie. Pet her, then jump on and take a ride.

The questions will continue in your head. *Is this the right time? Can I afford it? Are the risks too big? What about my other obligations?* Reasonable questions, one and all, but they should not stop you. That seems so clear to me now, but years ago I wasn't so sure. I owe my mother for helping me through these questions.

I was sitting on the couch crying when the phone rang.

"Hey," was all I could muster. I had called my mother an hour earlier, and now she was getting back to me.

She could hear it in my voice. "What's wrong, babe?"

"I think it's time to leave Ernst & Young," I replied.

She knew I was not happy. I loved business. I was fascinated with relationships and communication, but I didn't fit in at all. I didn't enjoy professional attire. I didn't care for small talk at the office. I didn't watch the sports or shows that everyone else seemed to watch. I didn't like being a cog in a big wheel. The list was long. I really appreciated EY, but needed to go.

On the outside, I had what most assumed was a great job for a young professional: above average pay, an interesting role, a premier company for whom to work, etc. People assumed I was happy and going places.

"I know you've been thinking about your next move. Do you know what it is? Maybe back to school?" She knew that I had loved college and graduate school, and that I had toyed with the idea of becoming a professor.

"Yes." There! I said it out loud for the first time with the intention of announcing my plan.

"Okay, then why are you crying?" she asked. "What's wrong?"

I explained that I felt like a failure for not fitting in. I worried about what others would say. I was petrified to hear what my father would say. I was scared of going broke. I didn't know if I was smart enough to actually make it. Question marks were everywhere and they crushed me.

"Listen, you haven't even hit thirty yet and you're already getting honest about who you are and what you want to do. It took me until I was nearly fifty to admit a few basic things about myself. Good for you kid. I'm proud of you. Besides, what do you have to worry about?"

I mentioned a few things, especially my worry that Dad would not be supportive. I feared he would see my choice as an escape from work, a place to hide from the world.

"Your dad will support you. He might not understand why you need to scratch this particular itch, but he will encourage you." Then she said something that kind of changed my life: "All of these things you're viewing as constraints aren't really constraints. They're just fears, and they are things you can face."

She wasn't always the lucid motivator, but that day she sure nailed it. Most constraints are imaginary. Monsters under the bed. Nothing more.

Where do I begin?

You've decided to make the big move, but where do you start?

Just start. Don't worry about mistakes. As you make your moves, or even find your calling, you're going to make mistakes. Even when you find your fit, there is a learning curve. Know that and get ready to embrace it. The faster you embrace being good, the sooner you arrive at great. That's certainly how it's been for me. Writing, speaking, teaching, coaching, making courses – I was good, acceptable, and average long before I learned how to be great.

So, just start. Now.

The mirror, of course, is not real. It's just a metaphor about a choice to reflect and be honest with yourself. Hold it up and take a deep look. For some of you, it will feel quite foreign. For others, it's an old friend, one with whom we should spend more time.

You can start with the basic questions we all need to ask, which I noted above. Let me help you get started with a few more. Consider these: *Am I happy? Do I know my purpose? Am I stuck? Do I need change?*

You may or may not like the answers, but you need to face them. No matter which path you take, it should be intentional. That can't happen without happily struggling with these questions, and the evolving answers you discover.

Ultimately, staring in the mirror only hurts at first. For successful people, it becomes a habit and takes many forms. There are many sources of feedback if you're looking for them. A mirror, audience reactions, performance reviews, comments online, candid advice from a mentor, relationship moments, insights from meditation, etc.

Self-analysis isn't always easy or pain free. However, I can promise you that honesty and insight always trump delusion. Once your initial bruises heal, you'll begin to see the real you more easily. That's useful data when your goal is to improve. Just look in the mirror.

PURPOSE AND PASSION

Money matters. A lot. It keeps us safe. It fills our needs. If we're lucky, it covers some of our less essential "wants" as well.

Many people think that having more money will equate to more happiness. As it turns out, that is not true. There are difficult human experiences at every level of income: health issues, worries and stress, strained relationships, pains of all varieties.

Having experienced wildly different levels of income in my journey so far, I will admit that stepping up feels very nice, at least at first. A new car or home, a new toy, a great vacation, no serious worries about bills – yes, these are blessings. But in terms of happiness and life satisfaction, money has real limits. In fact, research suggests that after about $75,000 USD in income, more money fails to produce increases in happiness.

It makes sense I suppose. Money doesn't buy you real friends, doesn't give you answers to life's mysteries, doesn't make you a better person. Hell, many of the folks at higher levels of wealth didn't even earn it – they inherited it, were lucky, road someone else's coattails, etc. So don't over-inflate the meaning of money.

If it's not money, then what is it that motivates us? The research is interesting. There have been many theories and thousands of studies. Scholars have looked at our dispositions and personalities, genes, socioeconomic influences, parents, friends, bosses, and other factors. The actual focus shifts a bit depending on the specific era or scholar. It's been called motivation, drive, job satisfaction, engagement, and so on.

The carrots we dangle in front of others have received a lot of attention in this conversation. Scholars and practitioners alike have spent a lot of time thinking about what we can give others or do to others to motivate them. The things that hang from that stick take many different forms: money, promotions, acceptance, recognition, etc.

Years ago, I was fortunate to discover one truly great answer to the motivation question: purpose. Purpose is a positive and compelling reason to exist. It creates passion: an intense desire to achieve your purpose.

Purpose is stronger than any amount of money. I'm not saying you shouldn't chase money. I'm saying if you want whatever amount of money you receive (or you pay out) to have maximum impact,

it needs to be attached to very clear purpose.
Purpose fills you. It makes you feel that life has meaning, that you're not wasting your time, that you're making a difference. These things are priceless. In a literal sense, when you have purpose, no matter the nature of your current situation, it will feel different, survivable, educational, and even uplifting.

So, where do we find purpose? There are a few obvious answers. For example: being a spouse, having children, or maybe in religion. You might love taking care of your family, helping others as an expert, or possibly being some type of entertainer. Who knows? It's useful to think of it as a "calling" – that which you were put here to do.

Do you know your purpose? Is it driving your life forward, the center of all you do? Why not? I ask people this question and the answers are predictable. They tell me that chasing your purpose is not practical. It is not easy to do. It is risky and I have others for whom I'm responsible. These are understandable thoughts, but ultimately, they don't move me. They sound more like excuses.

True, one's purpose isn't always clear. In that case, I ask, what are you doing to find your purpose, or to create purpose? This requires questioning, openness and honesty, experimenting and exploring. Most people don't enjoy the ambiguity associated with the search. To me, it's somewhat shocking, but they often accept life without strong purpose.

In this regard, I've been incredibly lucky. As a young adult, I knew that I found business and relationships very interesting. At almost thirty years of age, I began a PhD program at Texas A&M University, resulting in a doctorate in Management (Organizational Behavior) four years later. During that process, those interests combined powerfully with a love of helping others. A sense of clarity exploded in me.

I knew my purpose. I wanted to be an educator, to be helpful, and to move others to feel hope. I wanted them to believe and dream, to feel motivated to become more, to see the proverbial glass half full, and to envision new possibilities. I became a passionate creator of insights, smiles, and inspiration.

This purpose manifested in a few different ways: being a professor, an author, a professional speaker, and an online educator. I find all of these activities highly fulfilling, but speaking, in particular, affords a unique visceral social experience. I get to embody the alter ego I created, Dr. Dewett, who allows me to be a bold and sometimes funny pontificator.

Speaking has taken me around the world. Many speeches, many beautiful locations, hundreds of thousands of people in the audiences. People laugh, learn, cry, and sometimes feel inspired. I get paid to do this? It's hard to believe.

Earlier this year, I was hired for my highest paying speaking event yet. It was a great event in Sydney, Australia. I loved it. I was able to positively influence a few people and my wife and I had a blast. Did I mention it was in Sydney? If you think this was my favorite gig ever, you're wrong. It was amazing to say the least, but it didn't actually take the top spot.

My two favorites so far were both pro bono gigs for non-profits. The more closely what you do aligns with your purpose, the stronger the satisfaction.

The first event was for the Houston Food Bank, here in Houston where I currently live. It's the largest food bank in the United States. The organization consists of nearly 400 amazing people who are driven to do something so basic and yet so beautiful – to feed those in need. The organization's president asked me to speak to the entire group as part of an employee appreciation celebration.

I was hired to inspire, but I didn't know that it was me who would be inspired that day.

When I arrived, the HR manager introduced me to the team. Then they gave me a quick tour and told me more about their operation. It was mind-blowing. Using over 300,000 square feet of advanced warehouse, kitchen, and logistics facilities, what they accomplish on a regular basis is truly impressive. The Houston Food Bank, along with 1,500 partners, distributes over 1,000,000 meals annually to over 1,000,000 hungry people in eighteen counties throughout Texas.

When we were done, they told me to relax and get ready in the back of the room while they opened the doors to welcome the employees. Thirty or so managers walked towards the big doors separating the lobby from the huge auditorium set up for the event. It was then that I noticed they were all wearing the same colored tee-shirts with pro-employee statements, such as "We appreciate you!" and "Thanks for what you do!" I watched in amazement at what happened next.

The entire leadership team lined up by the doors. They formed two lines, one on each side of the door, forming a long corridor through which the entering employees had to walk. Then, one of them picked up a big box and began passing out pom-poms. For a split second I thought it might be silly. I was so wrong.

At the designated time, the doors opened. Hundreds of smiling employees began strolling into the room. They seemed happy and excited, but the managers were far more excited. They cheered. They waved their pom-poms. They greeted people by name. They said thank you. They high-fived. As the employees walked through the human corridor, you could sense that they were genuinely touched.

It was apparent to me that the gesture was authentic. The managers really wanted to say thank you. They were not acting like they cared – they really cared. You could feel the emotions. It was terribly simple, but ridiculously powerful. It had impact.

After all of the employees had entered and found a seat at one of the tables, the management team sat down. I'd seen this many times before and every other time the managers all sat together. Not that day at the Houston Food Bank. They scattered around the room and sat among the staff. It felt natural, comfortable, and unrehearsed.

I know they're not perfect, but relative to what I normally see, they get it. This team leads with both their heads and hearts. I've gotten to know a bit about them since that initial engagement, and I've been back for another performance for a slightly different group. They are super leaders. How else can you possibly explain such a world class organization functioning for so many years using low paid managers and a staff that is mostly volunteer?

I might have made an impression on a few of them that day, but it was nothing like the impression they made on me. What drives them? Purpose. Through many conversations, I learned about their dedication. They are driven, obsessed, and completely filled with a desire to stop hunger. That is the beauty of purpose: it gives you passion and energy to get the work done.

My other favorite event required me to go to prison. Thankfully, I did not have to commit a crime in order to get there. The good folks at Prison Fellowship asked me to be there. They are a Christian organization dedicated to sharing the gospel with inmates. They also run programs in many prisons designed to prepare soon-to-be released men to reenter society successfully. Good people doing good work.

One prison in particular, the Carol Vance Unit of the Texas Department of Criminal Justice, is fully dedicated to working with the team at Prison Fellowship. Every inmate at that location is on board and part of their program. In fact, it's a requirement – they can only be part of that unit if they are part of the Prison Fellowship program.

I was invited along with other guests to visit the unit and see how they operate firsthand. It was delightful. They had programs teaching small business and entrepreneurship skills, a Toastmasters group dedicated to helping people build speaking skills, a library of donated educational resources, many types of counseling, support groups for those about to re-enter civilian life, and much more.

I must admit, it was intimidating to see the inmates walking around. Many of them had been violent offenders. Most were just people who were busted after one or two bad decisions. I felt I had to be there. I thought about the several times I was busted for stupid or illegal shenanigans when I was young and allowed to go free. I was let go for different reasons: the police knew me, I was white and privileged, it was just a different era, etc. I thought the obvious – there but for the grace of God go I.

The highlight of the trip was a big weekly community meeting. All inmates and much of the staff, along with all visitors were seated in the prison's large cafeteria. Darryl, the Prison Fellowship on-site program manager, a former inmate at that very prison, updated everyone on various programs and holidays, thanked the visitors, and then handed off to a group of inmates. What followed were funny skits, live musical performances, and testimonials – all delivered by inmates. It was emotionally powerful.

I remember thinking that I felt like a fish out of water. I was happy that I was not speaking to the group. After his opening remarks, Darryl assumed a position standing next to me in the back of the room.

He looked at me and saw me smiling and enjoying myself. "You're a speaker, right? You want to go speak to the group?"

"Now?" I asked, realizing he had probably planned this all along.

He nodded affirmatively.

I reacted instinctively. "Okay. Sure." Then I immediately thought, "What did I just do?" No prep before the event. No time to gather myself now. No idea exactly what to say. My nerves went crazy for a moment.

"I'll go up and introduce you after the band is done," he said.

I nodded and began thinking and sweating. What will I say? Stories! I realized the obvious – I'm a storyteller. I quickly chose one that I felt would appeal to this audience. It's one of my older stories. People love it. It's called *Paxon and the Gold Medal*. It was a standout chapter in my first book of stories, Show Your Ink.

Two or three minutes later, Darryl jogged to the front of the room while the applause died down for the band. He grabbed the mic and told the gathered hundreds that one of the guests would like to speak. He gave a very quick bio and asked me to come up. The applause was immediate and loud. It had nothing to do with me and everything to do with their enthusiasm for the day, the event, and how much they appreciated visitors.

We were now eyeball to eyeball. Me and nearly three hundred and fifty men in white prison uniforms, brimming with black tattoos. I was sweating a bit. I had noticed the tattoos before, but wow – this time they really stood out. My arms are almost sleeved, but believe me when I tell you that I had fewer tattoos than most people in the audience. Skulls, faces, necks, hands – no flesh was spared. Yet somehow, they looked eager and happy, not menacing in the least.

Like my friends at the food bank, they had purpose. Their purpose was to become a better version of themselves and to become a valuable member of society. They had a conviction far stronger than the one that put them in a cell.

Religion was the medium through which they were accomplishing this goal.

I took a breath and began speaking. Thankfully, the story captured them. It's one that allows me to be vulnerable by showing my love for one of my sons. It's about a lesson a great teacher taught my son, Paxon, when he was in the second grade. Things were going well about two thirds of the way through the story when the first surprise came.

The big climax in the story is when Paxon earns a gift card from his teacher thanks to his strong performance on a difficult math test. He had to work very hard over many weeks to earn the reward. He wanted it for its own sake, because he wanted to achieve his goal (a perfect score on the test), and because he wanted to impress his father.

They were so happy for Pax when I announced what he'd accomplished, they jumped to their feet and cheered! The story wasn't over, but they were ready to clap anyway.

I paused and took it in. I'd never seen this before. I waited a moment and then motioned for them to sit. I wrapped up the story for another few minutes and described how Pax was dripping with joy as he shared his achievement with me later that day. I quickly summarized a few main points and thanked them. I told them I'd never had so much fun working for free and that I was grateful to be with them. I was about to say a final thank you and walk away, but they weren't having it.

They all stood again and clapped and cheered. I walked down the main isle towards the back of the room, receiving enthusiastic high fives the entire way. Their passion spilled over on me. Emotions are contagious that way. They lived out loud with their positive beliefs and optimism.

Darryl shook my hand and said, "I guess you are a speaker."

I grinned. After the meeting, I took some pictures, signed some books, and gave them to a few inmates. It was a hell of a day. As I thought about it on the drive home, it brought me to tears.

I can hear you now. Some of you are thinking, "All jobs and roles don't have purpose Todd! Not all managers have the power to help others feel purpose either."

I say to you respectfully: you're wrong.

All jobs have value, and in that value, purpose can be seen. It's your job to see it, articulate it, bring it to life, and show gratitude for it.

Maybe you manage a group of sanitation engineers (aka, garbage collectors) – there is purpose to be seen in that role. They make the community better, cleaner, safer. Show them pictures of garbage strikes around the world that have happened in the past. That will make purpose clear quickly. What else might you do to connect them to the value they add?

Let's say you manage a team of paper pushers at a bank who support the mortgage process – there is purpose to be found in that work. Show them pictures of the new homeowners they helped standing in front of their new homes. Maybe you create a video starring an elated and thankful couple. How else can you connect them to the purpose they serve?

My favorite example involves a team of purchasing professionals who worked on a large military base. They bought many of the tools and materials that directly supported certain planes in the US Air Force. Their manager was one of my students and shared the example in class. The team lived in cubes, piled high with forms. Form after form to be filled out, day after day. It was important but boring work, until the day he invited two fighter pilots to meet the team. They showed up in their flight suits, helmets in hand, to offer a genuine thank you. The team never saw their work as particularly boring again. Purpose.

Money is great. If you hear someone say money can't buy happiness, you might be listening to a person who doesn't have much money. It's great, but it has clear limits. Research suggests that many things are more important to most employees. These include inclusion in decision making, good relationships with colleagues, autonomy to work as they see fit, bosses they believe in, and many other factors.

However, all of them fail in comparison to the one thing capable of turning nearly any task into a worthy endeavor – purpose. It's free. It creates a driving passion inside of you. It's yours to discover and use. What's your purpose? Find it, and you'll never work a day in your life.

SACRIFICE AND PERSPECTIVE

Success is never free, nor is it linear. That's why a focus on sacrifice and perspective is so necessary. In school, at work, or at home, these truths almost always apply. I'll go further. Success without big costs and sacrifice is dangerous. It's so statistically abnormal that it skews your perception, dampening the very drive needed for the next success.

Any achiever knows what I'm talking about. Any entrepreneur, anyone who has played organized sports, anyone who has been a parent, and especially anyone who's managed others. You naturally see ups and downs, delays, unexpected outcomes, setbacks, etc., on the path to an eventual win. There are costs. There are sacrifices.

Sometimes we fool ourselves into believing otherwise. Take, for example, the work-life balance movement. It exists because of a very real issue – too many people work too many hours! So the simple prescription is to work less. Easy, right?

Not really. For most professionals this isn't easy to achieve. High level success, with very few exceptions, will require a lot of hours on the job. Which brings us back to sacrifice and perspective.

When you really value your work, you can become blinded by purpose. Time spent working is a worthy investment. The sacrifices you make aren't really sacrifices in the ugly sense of the word at all. They are alternate investments you choose. You face an opportunity cost with forms of leisure and work, and work wins quite often.

Maybe you are coming home late a lot lately. Or, you're working quite a few weekends. Maybe it's excessive travel and missing kids' birthdays and sporting events. Are these your preferences? Trick question – yes! Yes, they are!

To Live Hard does not mean you can have it all. Literally, no one can. You can, however, live fully. That requires you to balance your priorities – but you do still have to juggle all of the balls. When you work especially hard or for very long stretches, you do so because you choose to do so.

Even if you might enjoy not traveling as much or attending the little league baseball game instead of working late, sometimes you simply have to make other choices. Don't tell me this hurts your family or any of your key relationships. That is a common notion that simply isn't true. The only time that is true is when you don't use what time you do have together correctly. Make whatever amount of time you have count.

It's a shame anyone is ever told their career success is harming their family. That is a dangerous misplaced idea that is sometimes true, and often is not. The truth is you need to think about balance, you need to work on communication, and when you are present you need to work on being present (i.e., put down that phone). You are not, however, a bad person – at all – for building a successful career.

In fact, your big investments help in a few ways you don't often think about. Your dedication to work shows your partner and family how dedicated you are to their success. For your children, you're modeling hard work and achievement as top life priorities. Overall, they see that you're creating opportunities for them, not just personal gains for yourself. So even when you're not actually there, you're setting an example. You're teaching. You're loving. You're investing. That's a useful perspective.

One of the most high-profile examples of people who understand this mentality involves the retired CEO of PepsiCo, Indra Nooyi. She's been a trailblazer for female executives, minorities, and in general, for anyone interested in success. Her brilliance isn't just seen in her career successes; it's also obvious in her candor and perspectives on work and home life. She ended up at #1 on Forbes list of the 100 Most Powerful Women, but the journey began in Madras, India and required endless hard work and sacrifice to get there. After various degrees, including a master's degree from the Yale School of Management, she held management positions at Johnson & Johnson, Boston Consulting Group, and Motorola.

Indra joined PepsiCo in 1994, and by 2006 she was named as the company's fifth CEO. During her tenure, she oversaw the acquisition of Tropicana and a merger with the Quaker Oats Company, bringing the Gatorade brand into Pepsi's portfolio. In the end, she helped raise revenues by billions of dollars.

She's very candid about the reality of the path she chose. For years while she was PepsiCo's CEO, she basically lived at work, and her family was a secondary priority. Her husband Raj always said that her priorities were PepsiCo, PepsiCo, PepsiCo, her two children, her mom, and – at the bottom of the list – him. Her daughters were known to make comments about wanting to see their mother more often.

She admits that with sacrifice comes some amount of guilt. That's the price you must pay, and one Indra felt was worth it, because, ultimately, the biggest gift she feels she's given to her daughters is a belief they can truly go out and accomplish whatever they set out to do. It requires lots of work, sacrifice, and perspective. Is there any better gift?

The example that hits closest to home for me is one that is a bit more widely relatable. It involves a marketing professional I met unexpectedly before a speaking engagement a few years ago. I was booked locally to deliver a pro bono talk to a gathering of unemployed professionals who met each week at a local church as a part of a job seeker support group. My job was to motivate and inspire them, but that day someone else stole the show and provided the inspiration.

When I arrived, I saw over 100 people in an auditorium listening to a speaker on stage. The woman speaking was one of the pastors at the church and the volunteer coordinator for the group. She was busy describing many articles and websites that might be of use to job seekers. I was to go on after her.

As she appeared to be wrapping up, she spotted someone in the audience and blurted out, "Sean! I didn't see you sitting there. Would you be willing to come up here and share a little bit about what you've been up to? I think everyone would enjoy listening to you."

Sean stood up and walked to the front of the room. He hugged his friend and faced the group. "Hello everyone," he began, "I'm Sean Taylor. Many of you know me from around town. I'm a happy father, a lucky husband and an expert bass fisherman." He laughed a little and continued, "Though I'd really like to be an expert husband and a lucky fisherman."

Everyone laughed. Clearly, he had done this before. I thought to myself, "I have to follow him?"

He went on. "I'm also a successful marketing executive with over twenty years of experience, and I was recently downsized."

The room fell silent.

"Through no fault of my own," he continued, "I went from six figures to no figures, fast. So like most of you, I've had to quickly adjust my perspective and my behaviors. After a few days of feeling like a complete failure, just sitting around doing nothing, I decided to get busy. However, months of dedicated effort produced no similar jobs. So, I finally decided to look for any job – any job. "

Heads nodded in understanding.

He stated, "I used to run a team of 40 professionals. For the last few months, I've been one member of a team of ten who clean offices at night. My building is 1500 Main Street, where I work from midnight to 4 AM. And, as of two weeks ago, I have a second job too. I've begun to learn the fine art of demonstrating food at the grocery store."

"It's been challenging," he said, "but I'm happy to report that I'm doing well. In fact, it's become clear to me how much I have to be thankful for. So far, I still own my house, I'm keeping my family fed and clothed, and oddly, even with two jobs, I seem to have more time to play with my children – so there has been an upside compared to my old executive role."

He finished his story which was packed with themes of surviving, sacrifice, and positive perspectives. It was heartfelt. He offered good practical advice – trade in the luxury car, cancel the country club membership, etc. The audience loved his short talk.

Following him was tough, and although my talk went well, Sean was the real highlight that day. His comfortable confidence and conviction moved me. It made everyone in the room realize that sometimes you have to dig down deep, swallow a little pride, and do what it takes. When you do, you might just realize what really matters, and gain the clarity needed to start planning your next move. Sacrifice and perspective are always linked – if you're looking for the connection.

About a year later I was lucky to run into Sean at a local shopping mall. He saw me and smiled as he walked over to say hello. He told me that he had finally secured a new position similar to the executive role he'd lost, but in many ways, he said the new one was even better.

I asked him how he found out about the position.

He said to me, "I was demonstrating food at the grocery store. While I gave away samples, I made the decision to try and chat with folks and get to know them. A few months in, I was demoing a new product and up walked a man who, thankfully, loved the sample he tried. Turns out he was a senior marketing executive for one of my old employer's competitors. He found out who I was and the rest fell into place."

I said, "Wow!"

Then he added, "Guess where my new office is?" He smiled and said, "1500 Main Street."

He had literally gone from cleaning the office at night to sitting in the office during the day.

I congratulated him and said, "It must feel great

to be back on your feet."

He looked me in the eyes, grinned knowingly, and kindly said, "But Doc, I never fell down."

I never fell down! Sean reminded me so effectively that day that sacrifices will happen and perspective is everything. He faced a challenge, and he conquered it. In his mind, he had not made an error. He made the choice to have a positive perspective and it helped him do what was needed.

Let me challenge you by suggesting that if you've become successful, you may have forgotten what it means to sacrifice. Sure, you work very hard and have lots of responsibility, but you've become secure relative to your younger self and compared to many others in this life who haven't had as much opportunity.

You can, however, rekindle a little of what it feels like to sacrifice. You can choose to delay gratification and not consume certain products or experiences until you feel that you've truly earned them. You can choose to avoid too much conspicuous consumption, whether that's a luxury car that's too luxurious or a perk at work that only serves to separate you from your employees.

You can also be a mentor to the young talent that represents the future of your organization. Share what you know. Answer questions. Tell them you appreciate the sacrifices they are making. Share your story. Become an effective listener as they tell theirs.

Remember: we can't have it all, but we can live fully. You don't have to regret the choices you make in order to chase success. Sometimes you show your love and support directly, and other times indirectly. In either case, long-term continued success requires more than just making the right choice in the moment.

It's about humbling yourself to make needed sacrifices. It's about allowing those sacrifices to be catalysts and learning moments. It's not about the absence of something you didn't get to do. It's about the presence of required investments and thoughtful perspectives that feed success.

FREE YOUR BRAIN

Your future success depends in large part on how well you set your brain free and achieve creative thoughts. You probably don't know it, but your brain has been imprisoned. Maybe it functions at a decent level, but it's likely nowhere near its peak. You are seriously lacking in creative thought. How much would you pay to be released from this prison? It's within your reach – and it's priceless.

We sometimes realize we need to take care of our bodies. Our muscles need proper nutrition and exercise just to maintain average levels of performance, let alone high performance. The brain is exactly the same, yet it is often the most neglected muscle.

We all want to be good decision makers. We want to be productive. We even want to be creative. In order to support these goals, we pursue education, sign up for various types of training, seek feedback, bond with mentors, and so on.

Let's be clear, though. With a focus on creativity, the goal is not to simply gain new expertise to uncover new facts. These are merely chunks of knowledge. How you access them and use them determines a lot about your success. To accelerate the process, you need new ideas. New ideas are, generally speaking, combinations of existing chunks of knowledge.

For the longest time, we were not focused on trying to make this happen. Instead, we held to the misguided notion that some people are creative and some are not. Thus, when you ask a manager or business owner about who is creative on their team, they invariably point to one or two lovingly peculiar people. Bob in Marketing, or maybe Louisa in IT.

This is understandable. It is not mean spirited or evil in any way. Just hire a few creative people and you'll get the creative input you need. This thinking dominated for a long time.

What followed was the emergence of creativity-related training. Immediately, the science and practice of various creativity techniques became clear (proper methods of brainstorming, "mind mapping," etc.). Unfortunately, they never became widely adopted. I believe there are two related explanations.

First, budgets are always tight, and other training and development activities took precedence. There is required training focused on culture and values, safety-related training, various types of required training from human resources, new managers training, and much more. In the minds of most managers, creativity somehow seems to be of a lower importance.

Second, I feel that when the impact of training is not fairly immediate, managers don't believe in it. The want to see cause and effect. You train someone and you see them notably improve. Creativity doesn't work that way. It's not about being creative on command. It's more about your brain staying agile and awake so that it can sense opportunities when they arise in your mind. Managers don't get excited about possible benefits at undefined points in the future.

I have long had an interest in this topic. I remember conversations with more than one of my bosses early in my career. They were all quite similar.

"So, you want to attend a workshop focused on creativity?"

"That's right," I'd say. "It's supposed to really limber up the brain and enhance decision making."

"Wait – have you finished the courses on the ABC system yet?" He would ask.

"No. I mean, almost, but not quite," I'd reply.
"Get that done and maybe then we'll see if we can afford the creativity thing."

"Okay," I'd say, while thinking, "You can't afford to skip this! It's creativity. What's that worth?"

Thankfully, a Harvard professor named Theresa Amabile changed how we think about this topic. Along with many others, she pioneered what is sometimes referred to as the social psychology of creativity. It sounds simple now, but at the time it was revolutionary. Instead of trying to hire especially creative people or focusing on training people to be more creative, we simply need to lead correctly.

Everyone shows up every day with whatever inherent amount of creative ability they were given at birth. The question is whether or not they are using what they have. What she knew was that, on average, they were not. People don't know or believe that creativity is valued and desired. They don't feel that they are particularly creative. They have little knowledge of how to be creative. Most importantly, when they think of being creative, they fear the process. They fear not having creative ideas. Even worse, they fear how others will evaluate and rip apart their ideas.

Thus, no matter their inherent ability, they chronically avoid creativity. A great leader will build their knowledge of creativity and its role in team success. They build comfort with the process to ensure that perceived risks don't thwart creative possibilities. Slowly, a fear of failure can be replaced with an appreciation for trying and learning.

This body of work sheds light on the many ways managers might enhance creativity. This includes how we give feedback, how we use goals, how we evaluate employees, the role of time pressure and resources, and many other useful ideas.

Possibly my favorite contribution has its roots in cognitive psychology. It turns out our brains can function in two very different modes. The more common is sometimes called automatic mode. Here the brain is simply following scripts. Over time, you have learned an unmeasurable number of scripts. How to speak. How to eat. How to put on your pants. How to turn on the television. No conscious thought is needed. No creativity required. You've learned the routine, so just follow the script. This aspect of the brain shows shocking efficiency.

In contrast, the brain is also capable of functioning in what is often referred to as a controlled mode. This is an awake, or conscious mode. You're actively thinking and looking for what makes sense. You're not following a script. This happens, for example, in learning environments, because in areas where you have no knowledge or established routines, the brain must stay very awake and active.

It's interesting that this work began to emerge during the rise of many popular systems of thought in the business world. In the 1980s and 1990s, ISO, lean, agile, and related ideas rose to prominence. All are important, and each made significant contributions. However, all great advances have unintended outcomes.

In this case, we fell in love with the efficiencies provided by the rules and structures presented by these business systems. We sought to reduce errors, to make quality repeatable, and other highly important goals. The downside is that we became crazy rule followers. An ISO system, for example, would ask you whether or not a process was documented and followed correctly, as opposed to helping you think about how to change and improve the process.

Efficiency ruled the day! Eventually many millions of professionals started thinking in terms of routines. Honestly, we've been using routines to gain order from chaos since the beginning, long before the rise of the systems I've noted. The benefits are immense: less wasted time, predictable processes and outcomes, costs controls, etc.

There is also a clear downside associated with a love of routines and efficiencies – especially the negative impact on creative thought.

Recall that creativity requires many quality chunks of knowledge free floating in your mind, willing and able to mingle and get to know each other. When they collide, creativity is born. Routines only ensure an efficient path towards one prescribed goal (e.g., how to make a particular product), but they don't help you imagine other paths towards other goals. They are designed to do just the opposite.

Our indoctrination into a love of routines begins at a very young age. It's required. We are constantly bombarded with endless stimuli to consider: the sounds we hear, the temperature around us, hunger pains, our thoughts, the things others say to us, etc. The list is impossibly long, so humans evolved to embrace scripts and routines so that we can subconsciously take advantage of our knowledge and experiences somewhat effortlessly. It's literally impossible to actively pay attention to all of the stimuli hitting you in any given moment.

As children, we're wired to be energetic, active, and questioning. Adults can't wait to clamp down on the rowdiness with new rules and routines. Slowly but surely, careless wandering and exploration are replaced by the scripts and routines needed to keep order.

Think about what happens to little Johnny when he shows up at school every day. Does he think to himself, "Hmm, where should I go? Where shall I explore? What interesting thing can I imagine doing right now?" No! He quickly reports to his assigned room, and sits where? His assigned seat.

Later that day, when little Johnny needs to visit the restroom, what does he do? Does he get up and quietly excuse himself? Nope. He follows another script. He raises his hand, asks permission, and takes possession of a typically large "hall pass." Only then does he leave.

Rules. Routines. Scripts. Conscious thought not needed.

As we get to college, things don't change that much. In fact, they get worse. College was once a time of fun growth and exploration. It still is, but not as much. Now you have to take the required classes, get a job for money, find one or more internships, and serve in a few extracurricular leadership roles too. That doesn't leave a lot of free time to think creatively.

You endure it, dreaming about the huge money you'll be making when you finally finish and land that big job. You finally get the nice salary.
It's great, right? Kinda. You also voluntarily take on a million new rules and routines. Mondays are no longer optional. Your boss has real expectations. The salary got you a nice new apartment and a sweet sports car. Wonderful. Enjoy feeling the pressure of paying rent and making payments on the car.

Growing up is revealed to be a predictable series of new rules, routines, and scripts. Don't worry, soon you'll get the promotion you covet and, if you're lucky, you'll be saved by love! You'll meet the right person, fall in love, get married, and then start a family. Pure bliss? Nah. Moments of bliss sprinkled over a ton of new crushing rules, routines, scripts, and expectations.

Your brain has little time at this point to even follow the scripts. You are now utterly dominated by unconscious automated thinking. You wake to the sound of the alarm clock in the morning. You don't ponder the possibilities. You just hit the snooze button.

In the shower do you ever find that you're still wearing your clothes? No! You follow the script and remove your clothing before entering the

shower. You follow the same routine all day. You wear the same things you always wear. You drive the same route to work. You answer the phone in the same manner you always answer the phone. You go to the same meetings and sit in the same place. You go to lunch about the same time, usually with the same people, at the same restaurants, and order the same thing you always order.
Are you depressed yet?

I'm being extreme to make a point, but the effects are quite real. Here is but one example as proof that many of us have a problematic love affair with routines and efficiencies. I was in class teaching a group of MBA students one evening, when in the middle of my rant about routines and mental scripts, a woman started laughing.

I hadn't told a joke or otherwise earned a laugh. There were about twenty students in the class, and all of them were as perplexed as I was.

"Okay, I'll ask." I said and chuckled. "What's so funny?"

She calmed herself as we all sat waiting. "Something you said just reminded me of my husband."

We were waiting with anticipation.

"Okay, he's an industrial engineer," she continued. "He works for a large manufacturer and his job is to study efficiencies on the shop floor."

It was an unplanned moment, served up right on cue.

"He loves efficiency. He hates it when anything is wasted, especially time. One of his favorite things in the world to do is to come home early while I'm cooking dinner. That's maybe once or twice each month. He comes in, says hi, and then, well, he just watches me."

We started to see where this was going.

"So, he doesn't help you?" I asked.

"No, he just watches, and maybe engages in a little small talk, but mostly he just watches. Then, when I'm done and serving up whatever we're eating, he lets me have it."

Not everyone saw it coming.

"He explains to me the various ways he observed me wasting time," she said.

Most of the students gasped, especially the women. He apparently followed her movements around the kitchen. He watched as she tended to the food in the skillet, got something out of the fridge, and pulled out plates from the cabinet. In his brain, he was able to imagine a more efficient sequence of activities that would result in dinner – and he found it amusing to share these thoughts with his wife.

I don't know if they're still married. I do know that, if they are, he probably sleeps on the couch more often than he'd like.

The course was designed to get past the rhetoric surrounding creativity and innovation and give the students a few practical tools to use. It was important to me to move past sharing the idea that they're all creative and help them actually know that it's true.

The most basic way I could make this happen was by getting them to actively shake up their routines and thinking patterns by engaging in activities that are not part of their normal routines.

For example, I had them write a letter to their much younger self, aged six, seven, or eight. Their task was to apologize for having the audacity to grow up and abandon creativity and that awesome spirit of exploration they all once possessed.

I had them look at their tables and write down words that described what they saw. Then we all laid on the floor, stared up at the bottom of the tables, and did the exercise again. The change in results was always interesting. Switching up your perspectives is hugely important.

Once each term I would have them line up at the door to the classroom without telling them why. I stood at the front of the line. I instructed them to all turn around and follow me by walking backwards. We took a slow, clumsy, hilarious backwards walk through the business school, collecting many strange looks along the way.

It was fun to watch them resist these odd activities, then slowly open up to new ways of behaving and thinking. Nothing made that clearer than the night I decided to mix up my own routines. I gave each student a handful of uninflated balloons. I asked them to go use these in a non-traditional fashion. No rules - just do something.

What happened next became legendary. I believe the result can still be seen on YouTube. A few students blew up balloons and threw them around. A few chose not to tie them on purpose, to let them shoot across the room like little rockets. A few others started a larger group conversation about what they might be able to do if they worked together.

They decided to blow up the balloons and fill an elevator completely, in order to surprise some other unsuspecting student. It seemed harmless enough as I watched it unfold. My thirty plus MBA students walked the halls, blew up many balloons, and finally arrived at their destination: the third floor of the business school. They planned to cram the elevator full of balloons, send it to the first floor, then run down the stairs to see their work in action.

I followed them. There was a lot of laughing involved. People stared at us. I saw the Dean at one point – he just shook his head at me. The students gathered near the elevators on the first floor, and as I joined them, I noticed something unexpected. An older senior faculty member was waiting by the elevator. He looked at my students with a puzzled expression, saw me, and then explained how his bad knees prevented him from using the stairs.

Ding. The elevator arrived and the doors opened. Balloons spilled out everywhere around him. The students nearly passed out from laughter. I contained myself as my senior colleague looked at me, vaguely aware that I was responsible.

Not deterred, the man with bad knees walked straight into the elevator, still half full of balloons. He kicked a few out of the way to allow the doors to close – and he was gone. Sometimes taking principled risks leads to unexpected outcomes.

More importantly, somewhat silly activities like these did for these students what Dr. Amabile and others did for me. They were mind opening.

Now it's your turn. Your task is to do the same for yourself, and then, others.

So, try this on for size: get up at a different time, use a different morning routine, wear different clothes to work, take a different route, schedule your day differently, shake up how you answer your phone, where you sit at the meeting, when you eat and with whom, what you eat, etc.
Don't do this every day. Try it at least once per quarter. On the first day, your brain might feel like it's going to explode. You'll survive, and then in day two or three, new thoughts will begin to emerge.

New thoughts. What a precious resource. It's time to set your brain free.

LEAVE A MARK, NOT A STAIN

Nobody has ever said life was easy. Nobody owes you anything. Ever heard statements like these? Well, in reality, things are even worse! Allow me to rephrase and simply suggest: life is what you make it, learning is the foundation of success, and learning can be excruciating before it's exhilarating.

Success requires you to adopt a new view of learning. You have to be realistic and embrace a challenging perspective, not a fluffy, pain-free view of learning. There are many "learning is simple" messages out there. These include advertisements, testimonials, scenes in books and movies, and many more.

These messages like to depict times where learning is needed, doable, pain free, and usually quite fun. Thus, the guy in the commercial learns the new language, the kid in the brochure earns his degree, the girl in the video masters playing the piano. Isn't learning cool?

The trouble with all of these depictions is that they are radically incomplete. Learning is ultimately satisfying for most of us, but to get to the satisfying part, you have to endure some amount of pain. Usually a lot of pain. Here's another old saying: "If at first you don't succeed, try, try again." That's useful advice.

Learning almost always starts with apprehension, question marks, and ambiguity. This progresses towards fatigue, self-doubt, and headaches. Next you hit the proverbial "wall" as you lose confidence and your desire to continue.

I can certainly relate. I've tackled and learned a few interesting things, but I've failed just as much or more. I failed to learn the guitar when I was twelve even though I had lessons. I failed to learn Spanish as I intended to in my teens. I failed to write good fiction when I tried writing a novel in my twenties. I failed publicly and spectacularly with a video training business in my thirties. I could go on.

When people endure one of these difficult learning moments, they usually show some amount of persistence at first. They try, try again – but not for long. The internal pain of not easily achieving competence hurts. The external pain that sometimes comes with it (e.g., judgement of others, ridicule) adds more pain. Why does anyone volunteer to stay in such a difficult place?

There are several reasons. For example, consider your personality. Some of us are wired genetically to be more curious and naturally tenacious. Social encouragement is another major factor. No matter what foundation we were given at birth, our fortune is heavily influenced by context. We might receive positivity or negativity from parents, siblings, neighbors, friends, relatives, teachers, and others. Your genes, where you live, and the people who dominate your immediate context have a massive impact on your development and potential.

Another huge factor is choice. No matter what you received at birth or how you were raised, the choices you make will ultimately define what you achieve. Goals and dreams drive us. They are the choices that present a finish line we wish to reach. They are the reminder we need that helps us persevere and continue when learning feels heavy. Choice is everything. The choice to embrace clear and challenging goals is easily among the most important in your life. It's a choice to chase purpose.

You will need this guiding light as you wander into the sometimes frustrating world of learning. You define goals. You chase dreams. Lovely. To get to the finish line requires failed efforts, false starts, mistakes, screw-ups, moments of indecision, hesitation, and many setbacks. Your task isn't to avoid them. That bears repeating: don't try to avoid them. Just realize they are normal and work hard to get better at managing them.

That means you have to do what only successful people really understand: choose to learn. Choose to persist in the face of challenges. I like to say you have to make mistakes, make amends, and make progress. You try, fall short, think, learn something about what happened, plan to do it differently and better, then try again. It's not about simply choosing to mentally move on. It's about facing the issue and using it to do better.

Make mistakes, make amends, and make progress! Unfortunately, most people find it difficult to adopt this approach.

We've vilified failing in most societies, and thus created a truly massive barrier to learning. People take failing very, very seriously. There are more than a few shady-looking characters we might blame. The shadiest are probably parents and the educational system. Together, these supremely well-intentioned people have created generation after generation of students who are scared of learning.

Possibly some of that is just the nature of learning

and can't be avoided. Mostly, however, it's about the over-use of negativity, judgement, and a lack of positive encouragement and space to explore. Kids simply don't want "bad" grades. They don't want to disappoint or upset parents and teachers. Instead of craving understanding, they crave the avoidance of uncomfortable moments. This carries over predictably into many workplaces, limiting organizations' creative capacity.

Thankfully, great managers know what great teachers and parents know: you get what you ask for. You get it faster if you ask nicely, find ways to be helpful, and model the way. You make learning survivable and sometimes quite enjoyable. There will always be people who don't support you, and moments of self-doubt. Choose to process them correctly. Instead of fearing failure, judgement, and scorn, choose to fear not evoking these things because you played it too safe. Choose to believe that if you have not failed lately, you're simply not trying hard enough.

I readily admit that learning can hurt. Sometimes it will sting and leave a mark. The key is to make your mark without leaving a stain.

Stains happen when we overindulge in misery, blame, and self-pity in the face of learning moments. This creates a residue that lingers and affects how you feel and behave moving forward. When the awkwardness of learning kicks in, you can make it smaller and fleeting or larger and enduring. The shorter the duration, the faster the mark fades. The longer, the more likely it becomes a permanent stain. What's the alternative? Avoid the awkwardness all together? Avoid failing? Feel free. Think and re-think a million times before you act. Always err on the clear side of caution. Bite your tongue and rarely speak up. Vote with the group even when you don't agree. If you're nice and bright, you'll still get a promotion or two. However, you're not likely to inspire anyone and you certainly won't reach your full potential.

Not me. I say try stuff. Who knows what the results might be, but at least you won't be boring. Come on – what fun is life without a little thoughtful risk taking, or even a few crazy risks? Just imagine the first guy who drank milk from a cow. Was he brave and innovative, or nuts? I don't know, but I'm glad he did it. What about the first guy who ate an animal egg. He had to be crazy! Sometimes you just have to scratch that itch and do it.

Sometimes you won't even take big risks and things will go wrong anyway. My wife once warned me that I needed house shoes instead of flip flops since I have the tendency to accidentally kick the couch in the dark at least once per month. I didn't listen. I had a huge gig coming up in San Diego. Bam! Broken toe. Giving a speech with a newly busted toe was painful.

Thankfully, I remembered to make jokes, share the story, and was able to use my predicament to help them learn. The injury left a mark, not a stain.

Another time I made a huge traveler error: I checked my bag on a business trip! Don't do that. I was headed to Oklahoma to give a speech to a group of accountants. I checked the bag and the airline lost it. I had to go to Walmart at two in the morning before a speech at eight in the morning. I bought jeans, a black shirt, and other essentials. I could not bring myself to wear Walmart shoes, so I wore my trusty flip flops. I chose to use my mistake to laugh and help the audience learn from my error. It was one of the best speeches I've ever given. Again, my mistake left a mark, not a stain.

It becomes easy over time when your mantra is make mistakes, make amends, and make progress! That's how learning works. Yes, you need to prepare and do your homework, but only so much, as action is what really kickstarts learning. Why? Because you can only learn all that you need to know if you learn to fail effectively.

Many organizations have become exemplars of this idea. Before the Mac became a powerhouse, Apple unleashed the Apple III, the Lisa, and the Newton – and they bombed. Coke famously tried to recreate itself with New Coke and failed miserably. Google Glass – nope. Cheetos-flavored Lip Balm – sorry Frito-Lay. All of these were big public failures. So what. They are each part of a portfolio of efforts, driving learning, pushing these firms closer to the next big success. Each time they made a simple mistake, not a stain.

So, when is the last time you failed badly? Come on! No risk, no reward. If you can't recall the last time you tried something and really failed, try harder. If your last big failure or learning moment was not within the last five years, you're not living life correctly. You're playing it too safe. Use this message as a reminder to do what I do and catalogue your errors. Take a few notes and create your own personal record of what you did, how it felt, and what you learned. Use these experiences and don't forget them!

I've had plenty of experience failing and learning in my journey so far. I recall taking an SAT-like exam when I applied for a job at Procter & Gamble after graduate school. My score wasn't high enough and I didn't get the job. I remember trying karate as a teen, only to have my butt kicked sparring with a girl in class. I quit soon after. I remember every single time I've tried to convince myself that running would be a good exercise. Total failure.

Of course, there is one learning moment that stands out from the rest. I was in the fifth grade and had grown to an enormous height. I was 6'1" (and peaked in the next grade at just over 6'3"). Predictably, I gravitated to basketball. I could block shots like you wouldn't believe. I played that year in the local recreation league and took my team to the finals at the end of year tournament. We were down by two points with one minute to go. Somehow, I found myself unguarded near the basket. I was usually quiet, but decided to yell for the ball. They threw it to me. I was elated. Miraculously, there was no one in my way – I scored with a flawless layup. Cheers erupted... from the other team. I scored on the wrong goal.

Thanks to great teammates, we came back and won the game in spite of my embarrassing error. The next game, I made the decision to not care when kids I knew made jokes about what I had done. I proceeded to block shots. I scored. We won. It was my first real experience with publicly failing and having all eyes on me for all the wrong reasons. I'm grateful to say it was also the first time I chose to make a mark instead of leaving a stain. No pity, no running away, no blame. Just make mistakes, make amends, and make progress.

Now you know. Successful people aren't without failure, just the opposite. They're just the best at failing. Now ask yourself, when was the last time you screwed up and turned it into something useful?

THE POET AND THE MEATHEAD

A primary goal for all parents is to be sure their children are happy and safe. If we're being honest, we also want them to be successful, though we sometimes wonder whether or not they have what it takes to be successful. It comes from a good place, but these assessments or judgments aren't always useful for the kids. Like everyone else, I learned this the hard way.

One of the biggest traps we fall into is reacting to perceived strengths and weaknesses in our children. They can be hard to pinpoint. Keep in mind that kids are always growing and changing. Personality emerges over time while kids evolve throughout adolescence. It's hard to know when certain abilities and interests will show up or how they will shift. That's why making judgments about what you see at certain points in their development is dangerous. At least, it was for me.

Take my oldest son, Paxon, as an example. This

young man is so smart, kind, and hard-working. When he was in elementary school, he surprised me with his resistance to sports. Sports might provide a context where his kind disposition could be a deficit. What? Kindness a problem? "Maybe," I thought. In general, he was a dream child – still is. Even though he was socially shy, he was terribly articulate for his age, tested off the charts in school, never got in trouble, loved to read, and was curious and imaginative.

In contrast, consider my youngest child, Parker. His behaviors sometimes scream, "Look at me!" He didn't test particularly well until the fifth grade. Reading seemed challenging. Initially, it appeared that sports would be his calling. For a few years, he was just amazing. In peewee football, six or seven touchdowns per game was the norm. His social skills were above average, so much so that he found himself in trouble a time or two at school for talking, screwing around, and fighting. He was not as curious as Pax, but was far more socially expressive – he loved wearing painted nails in elementary school just to get attention from the girls.

I love those boys, so much so that I had to give them nicknames. Pax was in the fifth grade. Parker was in the first grade. I don't want to over-simplify them, but the labels seemed obvious. I called them the poet (Paxon) and the meathead (Parker).

Crude, colorful, funny, somewhat accurate – for whatever reason these are the names that stuck in my head. Their mom was not impressed, but the neighbors and my friends thought it was hilarious. One night I was thinking about their future. Honest thoughts. Tough thoughts. However, looking back, I'm not sure how accurate they were. When I thought about Pax, there was so much to be proud of, but I questioned whether or not he would be an effective leader. At the time, I was still a professor and this was allegedly my area of expertise. I worried that shyness might hurt him. I knew with certainty that others would see him as the ultimate teammate. But could he lead?

Parker elicited different thoughts. I worried that he would have too much fun to be effective. He loved attention and I wondered whether or not that would lead to questionable decision making. In terms of leadership, he seemed like the type to step up and make the call. He seemed like a person others would follow. Great, but would he be careful enough in his analysis or just shoot from the hip? Would he seek only glory, or also the thoughtful development of others? More to the point – would he stay out of trouble?

I'm thrilled to report they both continue to thrive, despite my sometimes questionable parenting. Pax is currently sixteen, a junior in high school. He's an advanced student, successful basketball player, a budding intellectual, and a massive fan of rap music. Parker is thirteen, now also an advanced student, breezing through seventh grade, playing sports, still being social, and...staying out of trouble.

Why are they doing so well? Sure, luck plays a role for all of us (e.g., genes, zip code). Decent parenting hopefully helped. Mostly, it's about them. Their individual attitudes and work ethics are solid. However, there is more to consider. For example, are they successful because they built skills in areas I once perceived as potential deficiencies? No, not really.

They do possess strengths and weaknesses, as do we all. Their current level of success however, for me, is the ultimate reminder that a person's success is about far more than just the individual. Success is almost always a team effort. It's about leveraging strengths through collaboration. It's about the synergy of people working together. It's about recognizing preferences to achieve balance on a team.

I was cooking dinner one night when a new thought hit my brain. Most weaknesses aren't really weaknesses, they are areas of disinterest. That's why teams are the key. They allow us to assemble an array of strengths and skills across people that are needed to get the job done.

Nonetheless, we've had a long love affair with

mythical iconic creators. The amazing loner, the innovator, the leader, the maverick. A lot of these idols might actually get too much credit. In truth, there is no Batman without Robin. There is no Jordan without Pippen. Teams are capable of infinitely more than individuals working alone.

That night their mother was out, and it was just me, the poet, and the meathead. I was preparing a simple dish: chicken breasts sautéed in butter and garlic, seasoned with fresh basil, with mashed potatoes and steamed broccoli on the side. The boys sat at the kitchen island watching and waiting.

I noticed a few things as I cooked. I generally tried to act like I wasn't watching them – but I was. Pax seemed content. Little Parker looked unhappy.

Parker's unease began when I used the grinder to add fresh pepper to the chicken. He grimaced, knowing that unlike his otherwise awesome mother, I would make him eat his dinner. It looked like he might cry, so I said, "What's wrong, Park?"

"It's dirty," he confessed as he picked the bits of basil and pepper off of the chicken.

Paxon laughed.

"Listen," I said. "That is just basil. It adds yummy flavor to the chicken. And that's just pepper. You

know what pepper is. It's yummy too. Plain chicken can be boring, you have to try new things. Young man, you need to realize that variety is the spice of life."
"I don't like variety," he whimpered.

Pax laughed again.

I served them and dove into my own plate of food, continuing to act like I wasn't watching them. I listened to the music we had playing, a mix of Sinatra, Tony Bennett, and other crooners. Between bites I slowly began to clean up the mess I had made while cooking. That's when I noticed what they were up to – and it was priceless.

Parker was cleaning "dirty" pieces of chicken before reluctantly placing them in his mouth. Then it happened. Pax loved variety. He loved spices, and he certainly loved chicken. He reached over and took a couple pieces of Parker's chicken. Pax knew that Parker loved mashed potatoes, so he gave him some of his. They smiled at each other, happy to be co-conspirators.

I acted like it never happened as I continued moving dishes to the sink.

Emboldened, Parker escalated the game. He diabolically dropped a piece of broccoli on the floor between he and his brother. Pax quickly dropped one too. Out of the corner of my eye, I saw Pax grab a few pieces of broccoli from his plate and a few from his brother's. He quickly tossed them into the nearby serving bowl with the remaining broccoli. They grinned at each other.

Alone, they may have had to actually eat all of their dinner as they had been instructed. Together, they won the battle creatively. They were far from perfect, but made a great team. Pax throwing the broccoli back in the bowl was brilliant. Parker was the first to take a crazy risk and throw some on the floor. Pax ate most of the chicken. Parker handled the potatoes.

As they sat and ate their ice cream for dessert, I marveled at what they had taught me. I'm always looking for learning moments that can be derived from normal daily events. That night, my boys gave me three quick insights.

First, success really is a team sport. Neither of them was likely to pull off this deception alone. Together, they were more confident and successful. It's the same for any business: you have to hire correctly, develop and maintain positive relationships, take principled risks in the name of progress – as a team. My sons' support of each other, and their quality friendships outside of the home, provided a great context for success.

They helped each other leverage their unique preferences to achieve a shared goal.

Next, chemistry trumps talent. Chemistry on a team is about trust, commitment, and willingness to help. These boys were all in! They were brave little rule breakers. Listen, Jordan and Pippen never had perfect teams, but they certainly had amazing chemistry. Chemistry is the magic that leads to synergy. Paxon and Parker have always had a strong bond, a connection they share, independent of how they relate to me or their mother.

Finally, great teams take smart risks. They don't fall into the trap of thinking that best practices alone are enough to ensure sustainability, let alone innovation. Jordan and Pippen decided to accept – and tame – Dennis Rodman. That was a risk! Think about Apple – they bombed with Lisa long before they nailed the iPhone. It's the same for groups as it is organizations. The status quo won't do: try, risk, fail, learn – and improve.

Usually, when dinner was over, Pax would help me with the dishes. That night, for the very first time, Parker decided to help too. He got down from his seat and slowly carried his plate to the sink. Pax and I watched closely, hoping he wouldn't drop it. I think he wanted to help his big brother after they had collaborated so effectively during dinner.

Or, though not as likely, maybe he just felt bad for deceiving his father.

Their creativity and bravado reminded me of a scene from my own youth. Once, when I was Paxon's age, my Aunt Donna and Uncle Wayne visited. With them were two of their children, my cousins Carrie and Steve. One night the adults allowed all of the kids to eat alone downstairs in the basement. It was me, my brother Jeff, and the cousins. I don't know who started it, but the next thing I knew, one of us was keeping watch while the rest of us were flushing nasty bean salad down the toilet. We were a great team. Carrie and I are still tight to this day.

What about your team? Remember to put things in perspective. Where you see weakness or shortcomings, you need to look again and see preferences and the possibility for balance and chemistry. In the end, your success is about you – and a lot more.

With a little luck, you can become much more than just a poet or a meathead. That's the power of us.

EMBRACING THE FUTURE

THE TRUTH ABOUT DIVERSITY

It's one of the biggest issues globally in business. It's fair to say that diversity will be one of the defining issues of the next fifty years. We've known it's vital for several decades. There are many indicators, from new laws and legal precedents, areas of scholarship, corporate programs and training, many pundits and speakers, and so on.

It's of obvious importance, though our progress in embracing diversity and inclusion isn't always so obvious. Historically, we were pulled into caring via much needed legislative breakthroughs. Then came the training. Mostly, this hasn't helped. Very kind, bright, and well-intentioned people delivered training that wasn't always easy to receive.

You're biased! You discriminate! You're a problem! I'm exaggerating to make a point, and yes, there is a great deal more to it, but – these types of impressions were made time and again. It's not surprising that a lot of people, mostly Caucasian, felt scolded far more than they felt coached. Research on the efficacy of diversity training is mixed at best so far, and some of it does suggest a backlash.

Thankfully, things are changing in recent years. First, and most importantly, the numbers suggest that much progress has been made in the workplace. Whether examining gender, race, sexual orientation, or other bases of diversity, we're getting better at hiring and promoting diverse talent. Admittedly, much more progress is needed. Attitudes and preferences also continue to shift, as evidenced by increases in interracial dating and marriage, who is popular in the world of entertainment, who runs for top elected offices, etc.

Back to our dear friend, training. I don't know that it's the catalyst it could be. The main focus in recent years has been unconscious bias, gender identities, equity issues, privilege, harassment, and related concepts. These are terribly important and practical, but they don't always feel that way to busy people at work. They feel academic, heavy, and possibly threatening.

My prescription is a little different. I think we'll accelerate progress to the extent that we appreciate how this all started, share our own stories to make it personal and relatable, respect that diversity challenges people, and finally – spend some time actually being a minority.

So, how did all of this start? About 20,000 years ago, when we all still spent considerable time in caves, we developed a few thinking practices that helped us survive. Unfortunately, after thousands of years of new and improved thinking, some of our old ways of imagining the world are still stuck in our brains, literally.

Back then, we had a much stronger tendency towards self-preservation. Why? Because life expectancy was poor. In fact, you could die any minute for a million different reasons. So, when you see anything or anyone you don't know, you have an adverse reaction. A feeling of fear, a desire to run, a belief you should defend yourself or kill something, and so on. This was basically functional for our species at the time.

Today, we have a lot of leftover inclinations we don't need. Evolution, while mind-blowing, isn't perfect. Thus, humans all have an appendix they don't need, men have nipples they don't need, and in more than a few ways, we think unproductive thoughts we don't need. I suspect a combination of evolution, changes in social mores, and advances in technology will rid us of most of these issues in time. Until them, we have to manage them.

Likely one of the fastest ways to help people let down their guard is to share more stories. A great human-centered story helps build rapport and understanding, far more than the most lucid recitation of empirical findings about bias in the workplace.

Take the topic of privilege – white privilege to be exact. Is it real? Yes. Is it important? Yes. Is it easy for people, especially white people, to understand? Not always. The challenge is that while all white people have experienced privilege, they don't know it. They think it's just good luck, something earned, the kindness of others, or one of many other plausible explanations. Why would we expect people to attribute various outcomes to privilege? We tend to make self-serving attributions, not personally damning attributions.

Let me encourage you to rethink some of your experiences. For example, in my life so far, I have been pulled over by the police five times (not including a few times they got me for traffic violations). All of these incidents happened when I was younger and doing something wrong or illegal. I was let go all five times, even though laws were clearly broken. I experienced zero repercussions.

How is that possible? What are the odds? Can any person of color claim such a feat? Doubt it.

That's right, I have tons of privilege – benefits I did not earn that were simply given to me at birth. I was born above the poverty line in a decent zip code. I had a mom and dad. I have good health and no mental or physical disabilities. I'm male. I was athletic in my youth. I'm tall. I'm at least average-looking. I'm smart. I'm Caucasian. All of these, and more, are immeasurably valuable in terms of surviving and thriving in life. I earned none of this. It was just good fortune in the genetic lottery.

I strongly believe that thinking about how lucky we are in this manner and sharing it appropriately with others helps people understand the issue more clearly. Then, walking down a crowded street while nobody notices you becomes something you think about instead of taking it for granted. Privilege ceases to be invisible.

Sure, my folks were a little problematic, we were lower middle class, I lost both of my parents too early, and a few other things I might complain about. However, truth be told, overall, I was dealt a very good hand. Sure, I have worked hard in life and made mostly good choices, but I certainly had some big advantages.

Our next challenge is to recognize that diversity is tough for people. History suggests that our species is very capable of hating and hurting others who look, think, and behave differently than we do. Given this central truth in life, it's amazing we don't infuse our diversity-related training with measures that address this head on.

To put it bluntly, diversity is awkward before it's awesome. This means we need to admit it, talk about it, and maybe even learn to laugh about it. All of us, together. Awkward before awesome – that's natural, isn't it? Before you tried a certain food that you now enjoy, you had reservations. Before you accepted that job you now appreciate, you weren't sure how to feel. Before you watched that movie you love in that genre you hate, you thought it would stink. This is normal.

It's the same way with people. Before you endeavor to get to know them, it's odd. That's why a little tension and conflict are a predictable part of the learning process. We too often use these things as excuses to denigrate and disengage. We have to learn to use them as the vital stepping-stones they are, connecting people who inevitably share a lot in common. It follows that useful training will include a little about conflict management and communication to help us through this process.

Let's not pin all of our hopes on better training and interracial sex, though both will be quite helpful. Our best bet, at least in the short term, is to find ways to experience what it's like to be a minority. I'm speaking now not only to male Caucasians, but to anyone who enjoys being a majority at work, or in your community, on a regular basis.

The root of the challenge is fear of the unknown and an overzealous desire to preserve the self and the group to which you belong. This is basic in-group/out-group psychology. How do we preserve a great sense of pride in our group? We denigrate – or somehow mess with – people in other groups. All humans can fall prey to this, not just some of us.

Try this. Get out of your normal routines and go be a minority. Eat with people you don't know, at a restaurant you don't normally attend, in a part of town you don't frequent, that serves cuisine you've never tried. Attend a different church. If you're white, go to a predominantly black church. If you're black, go to a white church. There are so many possibilities.

By choice and by chance, I've been lucky to have these experiences a few different times. First, as a young person playing competitive basketball, I experienced huge socioeconomic and racial diversity. Sports often bring the poor and the wealthy together. Later, as an adult, I attended a very high quality PhD program at Texas A&M University. Let's just say there were many more people in the program who spoke English as a second language compared to those of us who spoke English as our first – make that only – language.

It's jarring. It's perspective building. It's educational. It's humbling. It's invigorating. You too are wise to seek out opportunities to be a minority. Walk a mile in their shoes! However, sometimes, it just happens to you. That can be educational too, and it's always awkward before it's awesome. The most glaring example for me involved a time I was invited to speak at a meeting of a national diversity-related organization. At the time, I was still a professor, only beginning the next journey as a speaker and writer. I was sitting in my office one day when the phone rang.

"Todd Dewett," I said.

"Hello, Dr. Dewett.," a man replied and introduced himself. "I lead an organization called the National Diversity Council." He shared how he had learned about me, that there was an upcoming conference not far from where I lived, and that he'd like me to participate.

I was used to taking these calls and was interested to learn more. "You want me to speak about some aspect of leadership?" I asked.

"Actually, I'd like to know if you'd be interested in being part of a panel discussion," he replied.

I'd done a few panels, and never really loved them. I always thought there was something odd about a room full of people watching a group of three or four people sitting at a table that itself sits on a raised stage. On the other hand, it was easy. No prepared remarks, just simple ad-libbing in response to questions.

"Sure, I'd be happy to do that. Let me check my schedule," I said as I flipped through my old-school paper day planner. "Yes, that date is open. Okay, so – the topic – what did you say? What is the session topic?"

"White privilege," he said. "Is that acceptable?"

"Well it's not my main area per se, but sure, that's okay." I said yes! I'm not sure why since it really had nothing to do with my areas of expertise. I've imagined ever since that he called me because someone else had to cancel and I was simply known to be a colorful speaker. I can't be sure.

"I understand," he continued. "You'll be paired with two other panelists who are directly focused on this topic. They'll likely carry most of the weight, but I want to include your perspective as well."

I agreed, we talked about the details, and ended the call. "Hmm," I thought. "This might be interesting."

Months later, I arrived at a city not too far from home, drove to the right hotel, and walked into the designated ballroom. I immediately noticed something interesting. There were over five hundred people in the room and they were every shade of brown you can imagine. Mostly African American, some Asian, some Latino. Best I could tell from a quick scan of the room, I was the sole representative of the Caucasian race.

I resolved to not worry about it. I figured I would do something I should likely do more often – keep my mouth shut and just listen. I proceeded to the front of the room where I recognized, thanks to her name tag, the woman who was moderating the session.

We both introduced ourselves. It was clear she was excited about the session. She was the Vice President of Human Resources for a prominent large company everyone knows about. We enjoyed chatting for a moment, and then she said, "Come with me. I want to introduce you to the other two panelists."

She connected me with two other men seated at the table on the stage at the front of the room. One was a renowned African American Studies professor from Georgetown University. The other was a well-known Latino executive at another brand name organization whose name we all knew, and then there was me. I planned to learn a lot, and to be terribly quiet. I wasn't sure how I ended up on this panel, but I was excited, and just a little apprehensive.

At the designated time, the moderator stepped up to the podium beside our table and tapped the microphone. "Hi everyone! It's great to see so many of you here for our session today," she said. After a little housekeeping, she introduced all three of us on the panel. I resolved once again to be quiet and let the real experts lead the way.

"Okay," she continued. "Let's get started. White privilege. Does it really exist? Dr. Dewett?" She turned to look at me. So did the other two panelists. So did over five hundred brown-skinned people in the room. They waited for me to say something.

I instantly regretted not preparing properly. The room was dead quiet. It felt heavy. I did the only thing I thought made sense. I grabbed the microphone in front of me, moved it a little closer, and then opened my mouth and spoke.

"Well, let me begin by saying what a privilege it is to be here." I prayed they would laugh. Thankfully, they did. Smiles all around. The tension lifted.

"Of course it exists," I continued. "For me, to understand the topic you just have to dive into basic in-group/out-group psychology." I gave a few quick comments about how we've being doing these self-serving and denigrating things as a species since the beginning, and so on. Quickly I remembered that my role was to be quiet. Thankfully, the other panelists and the audience joined in and I mostly faded into the background.

To this day, I don't know why she felt it was smart to begin our session in that manner. No doubt it was memorable. Since I was good on my feet, and a bit lucky, it all worked out quite well. Still, it was odd.

It was also ridiculously educational. I felt on the spot, overly examined, heavily judged, out of place, a little threatened, and misunderstood. To my minority friends – does this sound familiar? I know that my fifteen minutes on the hot seat can never compare to a lifetime of what you've faced, but it sure gave me a tiny glimpse.

You'll notice I've not spent time extolling the benefits of diversity. I feel they are self-evident. Better decision-making, more creativity, more needed empathy and sensitivity, and a feeling of being part of a richer experience. Truly massive benefits. These are fairly well understood, uncontroversial, and amazing. Where we get stuck is still at the front end of the process.

We need to get real about how to break the ice and kickstart more progress in this area. That means training that humanizes and uplifts; thus the need to use real stories, to learn to talk more openly about our own privileges, and to actively seek opportunities to be in the minority.

That's just a start, I know. However, it's human, positive, and makes learning relatable. Over the next few decades training will continue to be part of the process, and done right, I believe it can help. Of course, over the next few hundred years, the discussion of race will inevitably shift further. Who knows – things might be better when white fades into a million beautiful shades of brown. Between now and then, we have a lot of work to do.

THANK YOU, FERRIS

Live Hard is not just a suggestion about effort and principled risk taking. It's a mandate to look at your surroundings more critically. The landscape is shifting, so you have to ask how you can use that reality. It's a time of radical demographic change, a massive step forward in diversity.

In the diversity discussion, we've talked a lot about women and minorities – and we're not about to stop – but, there is a group we need to talk about that I feel has been somewhat neglected – young people.

Male, female, or otherwise; white, black, brown, or purple – the demographers tell us that young people will soon be taking over in massive proportions. The only question is, "Are you ready?"

When people look at young talent, the conversation often becomes focused on the need for "seasoning." Sure, the young lack experience, but this is an incomplete observation. This view blinds us to the true value of young talent. They have the most eager minds, the most vibrant capacity to dream, the biggest willingness to take principled risks, and the greatest interest in overturning outdated conventions.

I suspect that telling them to wait their turn has always been about power as much as experience. People with power don't want to give it up. So, while waiting for the often hard to define "seasoning," we've missed out on a fair amount of great thinking!

Let's be clear. With few exceptions, artists, scientists, and entrepreneurs all make their greatest contributions early in their careers, often very early. What does this suggest about what we've been missing in organizational life by keeping the young down? It suggests we've been missing out on a lot.

Many varieties of thinkers have long espoused the power of youth. More than a few managers have too. One of my favorite examples is John Hughes, the beloved filmmaker. Many of the characters he created, or helped create, really do exemplify the passion, the imagination, the intellect, and the bravado of young people.

Mr. Hughes was one the greatest creators of fun, insightful movies ever. Maybe you've heard of some his work: *The Breakfast Club, Pretty in Pink, Sixteen Candles, Weird Science,* and *Some Kind of Wonderful,* just to name a few.

I dare you to try to live up to the ideals of those memorable characters. In fact, your career might depend on it.

Andie Walsh, in the movie *Pretty in Pink*, said, "If somebody doesn't believe in me, I can't believe in them." So, here's your opportunity. As the mass retirement of the boomers commences, how fast and how genuinely will you build bridges with the next generation who will run your organizations?

I mean, if not now, then when? Keith Nelson, in *Some Kind of Wonderful*, said to his father, "Then I'm nineteen, then I'm twenty, when does my life belong to me?" He was tired of his dad telling him how to live. Sound familiar to any of you? It's not terribly different than one generation of management telling the next how to manage, and how to do things "right."

Duckie, from *Pretty in Pink*, said, "Whether or not you face the future, it happens." And Cameron, from *Ferris Bueller's Day Off*, stated, "I'm not going to sit on my ass as the events that affect me unfold to determine the course of my life. I'm going to take a stand." So, do you want to argue with the next generation about seasoning, or help them get it as soon as possible?

We always seem to be talking about change and the increasing pace with which change is affecting our organizations. Well, the young are wired to embrace change and growth. How can helping them be successful not be our number one workforce priority moving forward?

Do you remember the closing scene in *The Breakfast Club* when Brian read aloud his short essay to the principal? In the span of one afternoon, these seemingly simple teens opened up their minds, raged, humbled themselves, learned, bonded, and matured.

The essay read, "Dear Mr. Vernon, we accept the fact that we had to sacrifice a whole Saturday in detention for whatever it was we did wrong. What we did was wrong, but we think you're crazy to make us write an essay telling you who we think we are. You see us as you want to see us, in the simplest terms and the most convenient definitions. But what we found out is that each one of us is a brain, and an athlete, and a basket case, a princess, and a criminal. Does that answer your question? Sincerely yours, the Breakfast Club."

Sure, my fellow older people, you might not understand some of them. Believe me, I get it, but this isn't about us. Your legacy is about getting over yourself and the team that got you here: what you did, what you like, what you value, how you speak, how you behave. It's about that next bunch.

The ones who, frankly, might look a little suspect to you. You won't like them all, so what – get over it.

When the principal in *Ferris Bueller's Day Off* expressed his disdain for Ferris, his able assistant

Grace set him straight when she remined him, "Oh, well, he's very popular, Ed. The sportos, the motorheads, the geeks, sluts, bloods, waistoids, dweebies, dickheads — they all adore him. They think he's a righteous dude." Sometimes we just need to remove the filter and speak truth to power.

So as you look for your future leaders, stop overly relying on your old ideas about what makes sense and what's predictive. Instead, watch them, and see who's following who. Then ask why, and show a little interest. You might be surprised what you learn. You might be surprised who steps up.

To all you title holders and gray hairs, I say to you that if you don't know what they value and you don't endeavor to move mountains to go find out, well, they'll judge you too, and when they can, they'll take their talents elsewhere. They rightly think of themselves not unlike how the great Ferris Bueller thought about Cameron's car-obsessed father when he said, "A man with priorities so far out of whack doesn't deserve such a fine automobile." With great respect, I ask, do we deserve these kids who will be our future?

The very same amazing fictional character also comforts us and tells us this transition will work, we won't get busted or fail, because, as he said to his girlfriend Sloane and his buddy Cameron when they almost got caught skipping school by Ferris' dad, "Only the meek get pinched. The bold survive."

In the end, I think we're going to enjoy this new generation. We're going to embrace them, and when we do, I think they'll pay us the same genius compliment that Samantha once gave the geek in *Sixteen Candles*. She felt heard and respected, so she said, "It's really human of you to listen to all my bullshit." Has there ever been a better compliment? I don't think so. So please join me, and together we just might save Ferris.

THE GENDER EVOLUTION

Which gender is better? For many years, there have been conversations, debates, and studies focused on answering this question. On one side of this competition, we have males, the dominant member of the species historically. On the other side, we have females, the upstart group clawing their way into rightful title contention.

So, what's the answer? The answer is that it's not a competition. Understanding human performance and progress is about optimizing potential through skill-building and relationships, not about one particular view of gender somehow winning. The picture that is slowly emerging is that gender takes many forms. Ultimately, gender shouldn't matter, and with continued education and advocacy, maybe someday it won't.

Sure, we've discovered legit differences, but thankfully, we've moving beyond them – slowly. We're realizing that gender is no different than personality or many other traits: it's a characteristic we possess, one we can sometimes identify, but often find hard to easily define. And – it doesn't matter.

One's gender identify is just another way we bring a unique richness to a situation.

Due to advances in science and social norms, gender is undergoing a new evolution that is leading us away from overly simplified black and white definitions. We now live in a gender fluid world, a fact that I strongly believe is moving us forward. Combine that with much needed progress towards racial equality, and we just might live to see what Martin Luther King, Jr. dreamed of not too long ago: a time we can judge others based on the content of their character, and not much else.

Having said all of that, I do admit I'm fond of females, and it's been fun coming of age during a time when women have been gaining a lot of ground. I've always loved rooting for an underdog. In fact, I was in high school when I first realized I might be a feminist. I knew I was attracted to women in a simple sexual sense, but soon enough I started to learn that I was attracted to so much more.

I was in class one day during the tenth grade when the teacher passed out a worksheet asking each of us our views on a number of gender-related issues. I filled it out quickly without thinking deeply. The teacher then walked us through how to score the worksheet and interpret our scores. My score suggested I was a strong feminist, bordering on being a radical feminist.

It was a one page worksheet, so, who knows about the instrument's scientific validity. I do know that I'm not a simple man-hater (though, admittedly, we are the easiest group about whom to joke). On the one hand, I have an inclination to enjoy female leaders, but on the other hand, I so clearly exemplify a lot of what it traditionally means to be male – look at me, right? Big, scary, bald, strong, loud – man!

But, truth be told, that worksheet turned out to be pretty accurate. I'm not exactly sure why, but I've always gravitated towards female confidants and role models. When I think about who inspired me to try to be inspiring, I think of a large handful of people, including several men, but most are women.

The people who taught me to live as I see fit, to live authentically, to be unique and not care so much about what others think, to speak up for myself and others, and to live fully and push boundaries – well, they were mostly women.

I don't have time to tell you about all of them. There are too many for whom I'm thankful. Thanks to Judy Jarrell, a professor at the University of Memphis, I gained confidence about forging my own path and taking academia seriously as a profession. Thanks to Sara Gardial, a professor at the University of Tennessee, I moved past mere confidence and began to actually become a leader of others. Thanks to Carine Held, a language expert at a firm where I was an intern, I added even more intellectual curiosity and open-mindedness.

I can't mention them all, but a few really do stand out.

The first is my mother, Judi. Without always knowing how to articulate it, she embraced personal evolution and independent thought in her own strange way. Nothing captured this reality more than when she changed her name from "Judy" to "Judi" in her 50s. It wasn't a legal change, just an adopted practice. It was an example of her asserting authority and claiming personal liberation. Against what, or over what – that's another story, but it was cool to see.

When I wasn't sure about a PhD, she pushed me to follow my heart. With regard to so many adult decisions, she pushed me to live for my ideals and to chase my aspirations. After surviving loving but highly problematic religious parents, she kept a promise to herself to raise her children as independent decision-makers. She genuinely wanted us to choose our own path, including vocations, friends and romantic interests, religions, you name it. For me, the mental space she granted me was the ultimate blessing.

Next up is Lorraine Jones, my high school physics teacher. She was a true original. Bright, funny, cool, and unafraid to be herself. Ms. Jones had a teacher's income, which she embraced and joked about. She never missed an opportunity to make fun of her Hyundai. More than anyone else, she stimulated my interest in education and in being an educator. She explained things in practical relatable terms to make learning relevant. Her students enjoyed skateboard rides, laying on a bed of nails, and all manner of silly, but educational, activities.

From where I was sitting, it appeared that she liked students who were dorks, geeks, and weirdos more than the other students (an orientation that later came to define me). Over time, however, it felt like she added me to their ranks. I was a jock at the time for sure, but I was also a good student, and I think she liked the fact that I didn't neatly fit a stereotype. Thanks to our bond and my ability to spin a book on my finger, I was invited as a guest to a few of her other classes to help her demonstrate certain physics principles (e.g., centrifugal force). She'll never know how deeply I felt honored.

Then I think about Theresa Amabile, an educator who is something of a legend. She is recognized as a top creativity scholar, having made massive contributions to research in management, education, and beyond. She was my idol early on as a young scholar. I nearly retired the day I saw that she cited me in one of her journal articles. Sure, it was a review piece and she was merely surveying the field. She cited nearly a thousand others in that piece too – but I was one of them! It blew me away.

Dr. Amabile taught me that my love of creativity as a scholarly focus was in fact important, when not everyone in the field agreed, by landing a series of articles on the topic in premier journals. She taught me that context is as important for understanding individual performance as any trait ever could be – an idea that became the cornerstone of my professional activities. She started as a chemist, earned a PhD in psychology from Stanford, and continues to blaze a trail as a revered Harvard Business School professor.

Finally, I think of Gay Gattis. She remains the most interesting person I've ever known. Born in 1899, Gay died in 2001 at the age 102, having seen three centuries. She was my father's aunt and part-time mom. She was a person of faith and lived in faith more elegantly than most who have tried. Gay was a teacher who became head of the Home Economics curriculum for the state of Arkansas when few women ascended to positions of authority in any field.

She was college educated, fiercely independent, and possessed a work ethic and intellect that scared more than a few men.

Why stop with career success when there is a world to fix? Gay voted, she organized, she advocated tirelessly. After retiring from teaching she began her second career as a tutor and mentor for young people. She focused in particular on disadvantaged and minority children. She was a progressive long before it was cool or trendy. My Aunt Gay was a profound example of thoughtfully minding your example. She was always kind, but lived very intentionally, even if you did not like it. Interestingly, Gay was an overachiever who didn't seem like one because of her passion for serving others. Thanks, Gay.

Fellas, don't worry, you made a big impact as well. How can I imagine life without having been touched by Scott Youngman's humor? Or how about Dave Gasper's mentoring and kindness? Of course, the biggest influence by far in my life (male or female) was Charlie Dewett (who was raised by women). He taught me the biggest lesson of all: more is always possible.

Is this rant a statement about the power of women? Sure. Does that mean I have some strong conclusion regarding gender and its role in our lives? Not really. I am, however, enjoying watching the gender evolution roll on. I'd like to believe there is a future where the topic matters less and less, though we clearly have a lot of work left to get there.

I'll end where I began. The evolution continues – and it's a damn good thing. On one front, women are making huge strides. I certainly owe the women in my life for pushing me and inspiring me to strive. On another important front, simple notions of gender aren't as useful as once thought. No person is as simple as male or female, are they? Labels are limiting. Removing them surely expands our minds and fuels our capacity to dream.

SAFETY, SUPERSTAR, OR REBEL

How do you build an organization capable of consistently innovating? Surely there are many answers to this question. At your core you need appealing products and services, a structure that facilitates progress, and a clear learning orientation.

Sounds simple, but any seasoned leader knows it's not. Everyone says innovation is essential, and yet few seem to successfully innovate over time. While there are clearly many parts to this puzzle, when I think about this issue, three things stick out in my mind.

You must set the right goals, reward the right things, and hire the right people. So, what's the status of these three endeavors in most organizations?

First, in terms of goals, we've made a lot of progress. For the longest time, innovation was a mythical creature that was noted when we discussed aspirations, but did not materialize clearly in the goal setting process. Over the decades, we've improved by including actual goals and metrics that speak to R&D spending, percentage of revenues from new sources, intentional obsolescence, and scores of related measures.

We've also pushed the discussion down further and further all the way to the individual level. Whereas we used to tell people to aspire to be more creative and innovative, progressive firms now form goals around these areas. Both scholarship and practice confirm this amazing finding: when you ask people to be more creative and innovative – they are! Of course, a goal does not make them more inherently capable, it simply focuses them on a specific desired outcome.

You can't talk about goals without also talking about rewards. In many ways, you do get what you reinforce. I'll forgo any discussion of how we often over-reward with plaques, certificates, trophies, games, and endless spot awards. However, when used correctly, rewards are immensely helpful. Again, both scholarship and practice suggest that rewards, like goals, provide focus, and also positive reinforcement.

That means if you value creativity, innovation, positive change, improvement, and progress, you need to show it with recognition and rewards. Amazing things can happen when we stop rewarding merely satisfactory performance and instead focus on both exemplary performance and impressive efforts intended to push us forward (great ideas take time, so efforts or attempts must be valued as much as the eventual wins you're chasing).

Finally, we have hiring. Our skill in this area greatly impacts our continued success. Unfortunately, this is our biggest weak spot. Historically, we used simple strategies including hiring friends or people recommended by friends, advertisements in the paper, promotions from within, and half-vetted collections of applicants from online platforms.

The real problem isn't amassing a pool of applicants – it's vetting them accurately. Again, our past practices were sometimes not so impressive. They included toothless reference checks, the standard "stick to the resume" interviews, group interviews, and the use tests (which are very often not valid or useful). In recent decades, we've upped our game through the development of scientifically valid instruments, behavioral interviewing techniques, and several other key innovations.

However, a big problem remains. If you have a pool of applicants and use good methods for vetting, you're still wasting your time if you aren't vetting for the right thing. Sometimes we try to evaluate potential future colleagues based on personality or disposition, intelligence, some aspect of a competency model, or particular work skills. Useful, sure, but let me suggest one missing component that might just be a game changer for your team.

You have to start thinking about the right mix of the right type of people. One thing we know for sure is that we too often hire in a manner that produces a safe, homogenous, and groupthink-prone team. The most famous research stream involves what is called the attraction-selection-attrition model developed by psychologist Benjamin Schneider.

The idea is that we tend to attract that which looks more similar instead of dissimilar to what we already have in terms of the employee base. Those who come into the organization and are more like the average employee are likely to stay and those who are less like the average are likely to leave. Thus, over time we, often inadvertently, become skilled at attracting and retaining clones. That, of course, will produce decent stewards of the status quo at best, not innovation.

Under this approach, an innovator is treated much like a devil's advocate. For the uninitiated, the devil's advocate concept originated long ago in the Catholic church. When the church elite gathered to debate whether or not to elevate someone into sainthood, a person was designated as the devil's advocate to intentionally question and call into doubt the person's miracles and good works.

They question assumptions, ask "why", and generally try to take down the opposition.

The idea crept into common usage over time and is now a phrase that simply refers to the act of providing a counter argument or view with the goal of testing the veracity of the position being discussed. It sounds like an obvious and useful behavior, right? Wrong. In practice within organizations, the devil's advocate is sometimes supported, but most often trashed.

Consider this classic research finding. Assemble two teams, each working in their own room. Statistically, they are nearly identical in terms of age, experience, etc. Give the same task to both groups (e.g., a leadership-related task requiring some form of unique decision). Tell both teams you want to see creative answers to the problem.

The single difference between the two groups: one of them has a person tasked with playing the role of the devil's advocate. That person is expected to ask questions, make counterarguments, tear apart others' logic within the group, etc. Importantly, the team members don't know this; only the researcher and the devil's advocate know what is happening.

We run the activity a few times, then bring in experts to judge the quality of the responses generated. On average, which team do you think is judged as superior? That's right, the one with the devil's advocate. This strongly supports their potential role in decision-making. But, all is not well in Decisionville...

After finishing these first few rounds, the researcher speaks to both groups, thanks them for their participation thus far, and then tells them they are about to do several more rounds of the activity with new problems to address. However, first, he instructs both groups to do one thing: select one person to be "fired" from the team. In the group with the assigned devil's advocate, who do you think they fire?

The devil's advocate – every time! Next, the teams run through the task a few more times. Experts once again judge the quality and creativity of the solutions presented, and voila – the team that previously had an advantage no longer does. They fired their secret weapon.

We love innovation but can't stand what it takes to achieve it – so what do we do? Consider hiring a very different mix of people, not just one or two devil's advocates. Real success with innovation will require a lot more than just embracing diversity and inclusion. That's a hell of a move in the right direction, but it's not enough. What good is it to hire a diverse group of people only to have them fall in line with a culture that loves the status quo?

You have to bring in the right people, and also make the soil fertile for growth. So, let me introduce you to your potential new hires: the safe person, the superstar, and the rebel.

"What do you mean we need to hire differently? Do you have any idea how much time and money we spend trying to properly evaluate talent?"

I was speaking to a client executive who was not happy with his company's culture or talent attrition.

I replied, "Look, the real problem is that you can't move culture by always hiring against your competency model. A competency model should guide you, but should not be used rigidly. In fact, sometimes you have to intentionally hire people who don't neatly fit the model. Your model reflects the average or typical person who has been successful. Great, but do you want this place to be average?"

"You're saying we've wasted mountains of money working on the competency model and then using it for things like hiring?" he asked.

"Not at all. You definitely need folks who 'fit in' and who have characteristics likely associated with success. However, great decision-making and innovation require a mix of people, some who fit in and some who, while very qualified, don't fit in."

"Qualified, but don't fit in?" he asks.

"When you try to fill a spot in your frontline management team, what do you do? I asked.

"Post in the right places, shake up my network, talk to the recruiters, and see what materializes," he said.

"So now you have a big pile of resumes, right? Then what?"

"You sort them into a small stack and a big stack," he replied.

"That's your problem," I interrupted. "The short stack is the small pile of solid applicants and the big stack is basically destined for the trash can, right?"

He nodded.

"You really need three stacks. Try this next time. Sort them into three piles. One for the safe people who are minimally qualified, one for real superstars, and one for people who seem terribly interesting but who don't really look like most of your hires. Those are your only three choices: safety, superstar, or rebel. Throw the rest away. So, let me ask you, which of these three usually wins the contest?"

His face scrunched up for a moment. "The superstar?" he offered.

"Nope," I said.

"Because they are too expensive?" he asked.

"Too expensive, too likely to make you look bad, too likely to jump ship and not plant roots here – and a bunch of other things hiring managers cook up in their minds to convince themselves not to hire a genuine superstar."

"So we need to hire the highest quality people. Obvious, but I hear you," he stated.

"And a few rebels," I added.

"Okay, how many?"

"Give or take, you need about sixty percent to be superstars, thirty percent should be rebels, and inevitably a few safe folks will round out the roster. The answer to my question, by the way, is usually the safe person. We avoid the superstars for the reasons I just mentioned. We avoid the rebels because they don't validate us, we don't understand them, and we imagine they won't fit in. So, the safe person very often wins. Is it any wonder we find innovation difficult?"

He nods, then asks, "What about the fitting in issue?"

"Did I tell you about the time I was sent to the adult equivalent of the principal's office?" I asked.

He played along. "What is the adult equivalent of the principal's office?"

"Human Resources," I replied. "I was a young professional, a consultant for one of the world's most prestigious consulting firms at the time. Can you guess the nature of my infraction?"

"Running your mouth? Drinking too much at the Christmas party?" He laughed. "Did you upset a customer?"

"I grew a goatee," I stated. "The managing partner for my office was offended at my grooming choice. He demanded that I learn to shave properly. It was the 1990s and not everyone had loosened up and become casual at work."

He continued laughing.

"So, yes, you should hire a few rebels. They didn't go to the right school. They look different. They profess an odd hobby – who knows! If they're smart, they will serve as a vital hedge against status quo thinking. That's step one. Step two is to constantly work to ensure they find your workplace hospitable."

"You mean we have to follow up and check on them, and maybe get them a mentor?" he asked.

"I mean you have to do all of that and more," I continued. "Tell the mentor why you're doing what you're doing. Makes sure they stoke the flames of original thought instead of beating it out of them to help them 'fit in.' Make sense?"

I followed up by telling him about the time I was hired because the person who was making the decision thought I was different. I was hired by a large consulting firm following graduate school. After a few months, the partner who hired me took me to lunch.

"Todd, why do you think I hired you?" he asked. If you've never been asked that question, let me tell you – it's unnerving. If you're a leader, don't ask someone that question! You can't answer it without looking odd or arrogant.

I thought for a moment, felt confused, then slowly spoke up, "Well, um – because I'm smart?"

"No," the partner replied. "I hired you because you're weird."

He went on to explain that he knew the firm needed "new blood." He was a smart and brave guy. Unfortunately, he didn't appreciate the need to also plough the land to make the soil fertile. I didn't fit in well, nobody seemed to care, and I decided to leave in a couple years.

You have to hire square pegs, but before they start you must go see their new teammates, their boss, and their assigned mentor to explain why this unique piece of talent has been hired. Prep them. Build expectations. Otherwise, you're asking for trouble. A rebel will show up, question things, not behave in perfect unity with the prevailing norms – and will be shunned as an anomaly.

That's one of the ultimate realities about diversity. Yes, we definitely need a wider array of races, ages, genders, sexual orientations, etc., but ultimately what we need is a diversity of thought. More specifically, we need an organization of people who appreciate a diversity of thought. You're wise to think about the traditional bases of diversity, but you only create real value by going further and working hard to ensure we all value a diversity of ideas.

When you combine the right mix of people – a mix dominated by colleagues from the superstar pile and the rebel pile – with the right structure and context (e.g., the right goals and reward systems), that's when the magic happens. That's when innovators are treated like teammates, not like devil's advocates doing something dirty.

Sure, getting there takes work, might test your budget, and will definitely force all of us to care more about improving our communication and conflict management skills. You have to get a little comfortable with a team that sometimes makes you uncomfortable. You have to stop talking about innovation so much and start building the infrastructure that actually supports it.

Or, you can just talk a lot about innovation and pray that the safe hires figure it out.

LICENSED TO LEAD

Leadership matters. It's a skill-set, not a birthright. Nonetheless, some people can't do it and should be removed. In fact, leadership is in crisis. It is a major contributor to the greatest health crisis facing humanity today: work. Bad managers are a disease that must be addressed. We will never reach our magical innovation aspirations while allowing the unskilled or unpleasant to run things. My plea to you: let's take leadership seriously.

On the surface, it appears that we've made significant progress. There are, in fact, many enlightened companies who deserve the attention they receive for their sustainable and employee-friendly practices. However, they are the exceptions. Most employees work tirelessly to merely tolerate their jobs. The primary culprit: bad bosses.

What's funny is that people love leadership. Over the last few decades, we've seen a massive rise in materials related to leadership. These include books, blogs, podcasts, degrees, certificates, workshops, coaches, speakers, etc. It's truly a growth industry. I should know – I'm part of it.

It's understandable too. The ideals are sexy. Supposedly, if you have the right mentality and do the right things, great things will happen. You will advance, experience big wins, and make lots of money. Your team will be productive and feel fulfilled. The organization will flourish. Turns out, these are all somewhat true. Research clearly suggests that organizations with more enlightened leadership practices attract and retain better talent, make more money, and generally kick more ass.

Because of its profound importance, our approach to leadership must be formalized. More specifically, it can no longer be acceptable to just allow anyone at any time to be anointed a leader. The influence that is integral to a leadership role is terribly powerful. Thus, some amount of thoughtful vetting should be required before giving someone huge power over others. What form this should take is certainly up for debate. Maybe it's required training, a degree with a sufficient leadership focus, a certification of some type, or a test for a license to lead?

Something would be far superior to nothing. However, people – tons of them – say the most ridiculous things when they hear others voice these concerns. They don't hesitate to dismiss the importance of leadership and callously resist any suggestion that leaders should be more formally vetted. Consider these common statements:

"You're either born with it or you're not."

What a joke. It is true that certain leadership behaviors tend to be useful, and that some people are born with personalities that naturally incline them to embrace these behaviors. Consider for example the well-known historical advantages typically enjoyed by extroverts.

Having said that, leaderships is far more accurately described as a set of skills. A skill is something that anyone can learn with the right effort. You can learn productive thinking patterns. You can learn self-awareness. You can learn problem-solving and decision-making. You can learn how to build productive relationships. Genetics can be useful, but that is only the foundation.

"It can't be taught."

I'm not sure why this one is so popular. We live in a world where teaching others to acquire skills is a common practice across untold areas of competence. You can learn how to do taxes, how to retile the bathroom, or study for a major professional exam all via different channels. That might include being mentored, being an apprentice, in-house corporate training, classes at a community center, private workshops, online courses, degree or non-degree options at a university, and many others. Leadership is the same – there are so many ways to learn.

Still others will say that you can't teach leadership because there really is no clear body of knowledge. Again, completely false. There is a large well-defined and widely-accepted body of knowledge. It covers self-awareness and self-improvement, emotional intelligence, decision making, communication, team dynamics, managing change and innovation, and so on.

To teach skills in these areas, scholars and practitioners draw on many facets of the social sciences such as management research, industrial organizational psychology, social psychology, cognitive psychology, sociology, educational research, anthropology, and more. Leadership is almost always a required course in MBA programs for good reason – the topic is popular, backed by science, and is essential for success.

"Anyone can do it."

There are many variations of this one: "You don't need magical powers." "Anyone can lead – you just lead." "Leadership is obvious. It doesn't require special training." I've personally heard all of these statements and many variants. They surely reveal how little some know about effective leadership. They are uncritical and belittling comments made by people who are probably not ready to lead.

In reality, not everyone can lead. Most who try fail. If you don't believe me, just look at the data put out by any of the major research organizations (e.g., Gallup). Most people barely tolerate work. One main reason is bosses. Most bosses stink. They stink so bad that engagement in organizations is shockingly low. They stink so bad that the consistent best explanation for voluntary turnover is bad boss relationships. Sure, it's easy. Anyone can do it. Right.

"It's all just common sense."

Leadership is definitely common sense in that you can and should rely on a few basic ideas, like treating people with kindness and respect, giving employees the information and tools needed to do the job, and paying a fair wage for a day's work. That's all obvious, right? Not really. Recall the engagement problem noted earlier, the lack of faith in the leadership of larger corporations, and so on – and don't get me started about the world of politics. Those folks can't spell leadership.

Having worked with, observed, and coached thousands of people, I can tell you with certainty that a great deal of leadership is not common sense at all and requires experience and training. For example, the intricacies of emotional intelligence, coaching and mentoring, dealing with poor performance, and mastering communication are mostly advanced skills. To suggest otherwise is to reveal you've never been a successful leader.

This is where it gets really strange. Not only do people say unfounded and unproductive things about leadership, they readily accept a more formal approach to vetting talent in any number of other areas. In these other areas, it's considered obvious and good form that formal vetting is required.

If you wish to be a doctor, you must have the right degrees, training, and certifications. To be a nurse, the same. A psychologist, same. CPAs, same. This is true for endless other professions. Thou shalt have proper credentials. To open a small business, you need a license. In many areas of the United States, if you are a minor and wish to run a lemonade stand in your neighborhood you must first have your parents obtain the right city permit or risk being fined (many versions of this are in the news each year). Even taxidermists must be vetted!

However, if you wish to occupy a role of strong influence over another human as a "leader", you need nothing more than a pulse. You merely need someone to appoint you. Sometimes these decision makers are thoughtful. Many times, though, they are misinformed, uninformed, acting too rashly to fill a hole, not properly skilled, or merely caving to favoritism. The average manager at the average organization has more influence over a person's life than their doctor, accountant, and taxidermist combined. Why, then, aren't we vetting them more effectively?

Do you think I'm taking this too far? If so, I suggest that you don't appreciate the true power of a bad manager. Sure, a great manager can boost your productivity, help you feel purpose, and push you to grow and develop. That's impressive, but not necessarily common. More common is the well-intentioned but ineffective boss, or the indifferent boss, or the asshole boss.

In my experience, about one-third of mangers are competent, about one third are mediocre, and about one third are truly terrible. Think about that for a moment. We have several million businesses in the US alone, and many millions of managers who work for these organizations. A huge group of them are ineffective and another huge group are doing damage to their employees. Why are we okay with this?

The competent one-third inspire me. They inspire their employees too. The model they provide maintains our faith in business. Sure, they still make errors, don't handle every situation correctly, etc., but those are rare incidents which become learning moments, and the net effect is thus positive. These folks deserve every penny they earn and then some. Employees fortunate enough to work for these leaders feel fairly treated and often move past merely tolerating their work – they feel committed.

The mediocre middle third can be a problem. Generally, they're not trying to be mediocre, but their effort and their ability within leadership roles are merely good, not great. They don't suck. We don't hate them, but they aren't admired either. Mostly, they are kind and affable without a real spine. This category has few jerks but does have too many people who are just occupying space without making a difference. With too many of them in one organization, morale will suffer, and innovation will fade.

The scary bottom third does real damage – regularly. Most people in this space should be removed from positions of authority or let go. They may or may not have teams with strong performance, but they definitely have teams who do not like them. It's their combination of unacceptable people skills and negative behaviors that define them as bad managers. They are only in power due to owning the company, favoritism or nepotism, a blinding focus on a narrow view of performance, and often due to simple ignorance (you can't assume, for example, that a jerk at one level is understood to be a jerk by people at the next level). This group crushes morale, harms productivity, and eviscerates innovation. And they're killing us.

We spend a lot of time in magazines and the press sharing praise for examples of great leadership. They are indeed inspiring. For example, Edward St. John, the founder of St. John Properties who famously surprised his nearly 200 employees with a $10 million bonus at a company holiday party. Steve Jobs taking only $1 in salary for years. Dan Price, the credit card processing entrepreneur who raised minimum employee pay to $70,000, thus changing many lives, while sacrificing much of his riches to do so. I love these stories. I just wish they were more common.

I talk to a lot of people in person and online about their jobs and their lives. As a result, I hear many stories. Some that are good, but many more that are just plain difficult. Consider these:

During the COVID-19 pandemic, an at-risk friend (due to asthma) was told by her boss that she was essential (she was not, she is a standard office worker) and must return to working at the office long before the virus was under control where she lived. My friend's teammates loathed their domineering boss, feared her, and always complied. However, on this issue, my friend fought back and demanded the right to work from home. Her boss publicly berated her yet finally, and begrudgingly, agreed. So far, she's not been fired, though she fears it's coming.

An acquaintance of mine who is a manager was recently denied his performance bonus – which he really needed. He recently helped design and administer a new performance-based bonus system. It was enthusiastically supported by the owner of the small business. Time passed, performance was strong, the manager earned a nice (but totally reasonable) bonus – and yet it was denied. The owner said nothing formally, but in so many words suggested he simply did not realize what it was going to cost him.

I watched a company owner stand up at his own holiday party to hand out a few employee awards once. The audience sat silent. Only his wife clapped. Two or three cronies quietly joined in. Hundreds of employees could barely look at him. He was unpleasant to say the least: sexist, unfair, demeaning, and wholly inappropriate. The employees were embarrassed to work for such a person, but needed the jobs. People with glum faces accepted awards they did not want. It was depressing and awkward.

I can't begin to tell you how many examples I've heard from women about men who have come on to them, stories about broken promises that matter, and stories of demeaning and unkind behavior. I once worked for a large consulting firm. One of our clients used downsizing as part of the solution to their woes. A particular manager who was targeted to be let go had a heart attack days before they could tell him his fate (he had no idea it was coming). The company sent one of their lawyers to the hospital to fire the man. You can't make this stuff up.

Maybe the most poignant example I've seen involved one of my former MBA students. I'll call her Elizabeth. She called one day, a few years after graduating, and asked if we could have lunch. She had been a good student and a pleasant person, so I was looking forward to catching up.

"So, how's life?" I causally asked as we sat down at a local Mexican restaurant.

She hesitated. "In some ways, things are great, but…"

I sat quietly and allowed her to continue.

"I've had one promotion, which is nice. My pay is definitely acceptable. I like most of my colleagues. The work is challenging, but I …"

She hesitated again.

"It's okay Elizabeth. This is just between us, confidential, so feel free to just spit it out," I said.

"I work for a person I can't stand," She blurted out. "It's not that I just lack respect for him, which is true, but – he's a monster." She immediately started to cry.

"He definitely hates women," she struggled to say.

"How do you know this?" I asked.

"He has said as much, out loud, on a number of occasions. He phrases it differently every time. Sometimes he'll say, 'Women are too emotional for finance roles.' Other times he'll say, 'All of this equality stuff is killing our talent." Once he actually said, 'If women were supposed to be in this industry, they'd actually understand math.' It's just the way he sees things."

Elizabeth worked for a well-known prestigious money management firm in the Midwest. The owner (to whom she did not directly report) wielded significant power in the area. He was a devout Christian and promoted Christian values in business, thus the story was all the more disturbing.

I asked, "Does your boss ever talk to you personally in an inappropriate way?" I was unprepared for what she said next.

"He has called me stupid, asked me if I'm 'slow', told me I'd be a better fit working for someone else, tells me to 'try to keep up' before he explains anything, and he smashes you for any error, however small, in the most degrading way possible." She continued while wiping away tears. "Keep in mind, this is almost always done in front of others. We have an open office of cubes and everyone hears everything."

At the time she was sharing her story with me, this behavior had persisted for over two years. For the last several months, her daily routine was pure pain. It was ruining her life. She said she found it nearly impossible to intentionally show up in the morning knowing what was likely to occur. Her husband couldn't really help. Their relationship had become strained. She couldn't sleep. Every day she would race to her car after work and burst into tears.

"Does his boss, the owner of the company, know about this behavior?" I asked.

"He's seen at least three or four of the outbursts. It's not just me either, I'm simply his favorite current target."

The fact that she was a strong, above average student in two of my courses convinced me she was being honest and accurate.

She went on, "I know that at least once, the owner talked to him because he told me about it."

"The owner of the company told you about it?" I asked.

"Yes. He knew that everyone in the company knew about a particular time my boss acted like a jerk. He wanted me to know that he cared and it would not happen again. To my knowledge, four of my female colleagues have received similar comments. In the meantime, my boss continues his toxic shit and talent continues to leave."

"And what are your plans?" I asked.

"I need the job. I really need it. This…"

She was in the middle of talking when it hit me. I knew him. I knew the identity of her horrible boss. I said his name out loud.

She was stunned. More tears fell. She shook her head, affirming what I said.

"I met him in Tortola, in the British Virgin Islands."

I had been offered the opportunity to teach in an MBA program my school had created in the BVI. I lived on a beach in a nice cottage for weeks, teaching most days, wandering the island at night. It was a cushy assignment to say the least. There were two classes being taught while I was there, mine and one other that was not taught by a professor. It was taught by an adjunct instructor – him.

I had one dinner with him and one night at the bar with him during our several week stay. That was enough. I politely declined other opportunities for us to socialize. Part of the time we were together he was kind, kissing up a little since I was a star faculty member and he wanted to continue his association with the program.

Then at dinner he mentioned his wife. He was delighted that she was into activities around the island he did not enjoy, so he didn't have to spend time with her. He talked poorly about how bright she was. He drank excessively and started talking about women in general in a not-so-kind way. I was very put off and quickly made my way back to my room. I distinctly recall thinking, "Jeez, he must be a pain in the ass to work for."

At lunch that day, we ended up discussing all of the possible paths she might take, everything from quitting to suing the company. In the end, we mostly planned how she could network her way into another role at another organization. She said that's what she thinks is best, but feels like a failure for not sticking it out. She felt like he would "win." I was just sick listening to this story about a great talent being treated so horribly by a pathetic dinosaur who was allowed to run free over an entire department. He was a high performer who really need to be fired or worse.

Stories like hers remind me that you really are part of the problem or part of the solution. The truth is we're in the middle of an awakening. For example, for years we've feebly embraced a narrative about workers making bad health choices. Thus workplace gyms, yoga classes, and obesity-prevention programs popped up. Now, we are realizing that the bigger culprit is work: excessively long hours, toxic bosses, weekend work, after hours emails, no guaranteed paid sick days, immoral vacation policies, terrible family leave policies, etc.

When you remember that most people spend most of their lives at work, it becomes clear that work is the issue. We see crisis levels of loneliness, stress and burnout, obesity, and depression. The physical outcomes are predictable: untenable levels of hypertension, heart disease, diabetes, etc. We're only now beginning to realize the true shocking size of the associated mental health issues. We keep getting sicker and sicker, while the associated costs rise at exponential rates.

There is only one solid conclusion. We don't need more yoga classes. We need better bosses. That's where more sane policies begin. That's where healthier employees begin.

Fixing our entire system is a daunting task to say the least. Don't fret. You can still do your part by doing the right thing. You can choose to be one small part of a larger movement in the right direction. You can at least punch the proverbial bully in the nose. You can call out the asshole manager and demand better. Do it in groups, not alone – eventually, they have to listen. I've done it myself many times. I recognize it's anything but risk free, but it's hugely important.

So, I'll say it again. Leadership matters. When done right, truly great things are possible. In the wrong hands, lives are ruined. It's best viewed as a skill that can be learned. It's unwise to let loose an untrained person into leadership. It's unethical to allow them to stay unless they improve quickly. It's really unethical to allow bad behavior to persist.

To improve life at any level of economic development, you must improve the average person's life at work. It's time to require the average boss to be properly credentialed. Technological advances are interesting and helpful in making more productive workplaces. More forward-leaning employee practices do inspire. However, there is only one best way to improve the experience of life at work for the majority. Demand better leaders now. Elizabeth deserves better. So do you. It's time to take leadership seriously.

A CALL TO ACTION

I hope you enjoyed the messages and see all of the take-a-ways, whether stated or creatively derived. To be as helpful as possible, let me focus your attention on ten important ideas you need to address. Get serious about bringing some of these ideas to life. Just remember that you don't have to make huge changes fast. The right first move will be different for each of you. Read through the following issues, identify two or three that speak to you, and get started. Soon enough, you'll tackle the entire list. Get ready for more creativity, innovation, change, and progress.

1. Articulate relevant long-term goals.

There is no perfect answer. It's about what you need and how you feel moved. For some of you it might mean changes in your personal life. For others, it will mean new professional goals. For many of you it will mean both. On a personal level, it might involve core daily practices, how you manage key relationships, or how you do or do not associate yourself with various issues in society. At work, this might include being a more vocal supporter of change and innovation, taking on roles within innovation projects, advocating on behalf of certain issues, or seeking leadership roles that allow you to advocate for more creativity, innovation, and change.

In any case, your likelihood of being successful increases tremendously when you turn ideas into goals. Be very specific about the outcome you wish to achieve, and when. Then work backwards to define the path forward that will get you to the goal. Don't stop there. Think about the people you need (whether you currently know them or not) and the people who may pose a challenge to your progress. What can you do to change or enhance these relationships to improve your odds of success? What about needed resources or new skills? Your plan should be detailed.

2. Face your biggest fears and assumptions.

Real change will not begin until you face the monster holding you back. This might include fear of losing money and not being able to pay your rent, feed your family, save money, etc. It might be a simple fear of failure. Who wants to fall on their face while everyone is watching? These are very understandable concerns. However, they are concerns, not real constraints.

You can't attack assumptions and fears until you name them. Start writing. After a few days of reflecting, what are the top issues that dominated your thoughts? It will be different for each of you, and there is no right answer. It might be fear of disappointing your parents, questions about your ability, or something else. Be honest, be specific.

Now attempt to name the single most important limiting assumption or fear. This is the one, more than all others, that stops you in your tracks and keeps you up at night. Say it, write it down. Make it visible. For example, put what you've written, or a symbolic picture, in a place where you will see it every day. Choose to look at it every single day. Speak to it if you have to. Tell it that you will not be intimidated. You will not be stopped. Say it. Mean it. Imagine overcoming this issue. Play that movie in your mind over and over again until it's real.

3. Determine what needs to be sacrificed or changed.

In terms of sacrifices, what is it you might have to deal with, delay, or let go of in order to move forward with change in your life? This might be time with your family, income, or material things such as restaurants and going to the movies. It could be your good standing at work or in the community. Few great things are accomplished without risking your reputation. It might last months or years, but what is it? You have to be willing to identify, prepare for, and embrace the sacrifices required for success.

There are a couple of perspectives to consider about routines with regard to change. First, to boost personal creativity, which routines are worn out and need to be shaken up? It can be as simple as your morning routine, the typical structure you apply to your workday, or how you use nights and weekends. It's easy to identify the more tired routines, but don't try to change a bunch of things at once. Be kind to your brain and try one or two changes. See how they feel for a few weeks before adding any additional changes. Overall, just a few per year will help the brain stay awake and focused on creative possibilities.

Then we have to consider more difficult routines that might be in need of examination. Think about where you work, your closest friends, your family, and key behaviors such as diet and exercise, religious practices, or any other big part of your life that you've identified as hurting as much or more than it helps. The biggest steps forward in your life often require other changes first to create the mental room needed for progress, but be sure to expect and watch for fallout. All change has expected and unexpected consequences. So, keep your eyes open. You've got this.

4. Know where you stand with your employer.

Stated differently, are creativity and innovation even on the radar at work? Is it mostly rhetoric, or are they serious? If they are serious, there will be many initiatives underway: efforts to improve processes, new products and services, advances in terms of employee relations, support for the community, the environment, etc.

Does the leadership team clearly champion change? Relative to most of your competition, are you making waves in terms of your bottom line, sustainability, philanthropy, and issue advocacy? There is no simple scorecard to consider, and the issue is complicated by the fact that what matters to each of you is different. Just be honest about the ideals you wish to support and whether or not a sufficient number of them are being addressed productively where you work.

Always choose to be kind and respectful, but find ways to have your voice heard. The other option is to find a new professional home. Either route implies risk, but that is the price of progress.

5. *Choose your best first target at work.*

There are different thoughts on this one. Some say go big or go home. Others suggest that you should use the small wins approach to prove yourself safely and gain initial momentum.

If you want to go big, great – what is the sacred cow, dead body in the room, or otherwise hugely obvious issue that must be addressed? It could be a technology that needs to be adopted for product competitiveness, a business practice that must stop to improve your community support, or maybe a policy that should be introduced to increase your viability in the market for talent. Just know that going big is the riskiest path forward. If you succeed, you will have a new stronger voice. If you do not succeed, you will have weakened your power on other fronts moving forward.

The path many find more appealing, which has a better success rate on average, is the small wins approach. This method suggests that you find a legitimate, though not monumental, change target and work to address it. Again, whether products, policies, or issues, the point is to take on a more winnable task. As you find success, your savvy and your support base will increase. More change then becomes possible, but it takes time.

In either case, you will find yourself in need of useful conversation starters. Improved conversation is very often the match that lights the fire for change. So think about a news report, an internal study, the article or book you read, the excerpt from the speech you all heard, or some other thing worth talking about. What is the right way to share it and use it to encourage new critical thought?

6. *Choose your best first target in life.*

There are so many places to begin, and the sheer number of possibilities often feels so heavy that people never get started. So, narrow the field. Narrow it down to one target. You'll get to the rest later. Start simple.

It could be that you need to make more money. You want to feel more purpose. You need to shift a few of your core beliefs. Maybe you have an addiction or problematic indulgence that must change. Whether the issue is your parents, your childhood, your sexuality, your politics, your religion, or some other issue – it's time to come out and embrace your personal truth. Change always requires you to fully face and address the past before you can successfully envision and create the future.

Life changes can be far more daunting than professional changes. It's not always a smooth ride. There can be significant feelings of loss involved. It's important to acknowledge this up front and be honest with yourself. You can get where you want to be, but all positive change has a price. In the long run, you'll be happy you paid it.

7. Identify the people you need.

Change is hard enough when you're alone. Bring friends! If you're addressing projects and issues at work that truly need attention, bring friends. If you're targeting change in your personal life, bring friends.

At work, success is almost always the product of a group effort. You are far more likely to make progress when you're part of a coalition of people who share the same goal. This takes a lot of work. It requires you to listen even more effectively than you talk. It requires a very strategic approach to relationship building. That means you'll advocate for some issues that matter to you, but not all of them at once. It also means you'll spend considerable time helping others with things that matter to them in order to receive their support in return.

In your personal life, you will have to think about two related issues. First, there are voices that need to be amplified. These are people who agree with you on some of the issues that matter, are kind and uplifting, or those who otherwise add positivity to your life. Work on building even stronger bridges with this group. In contrast, there are voices that need to be quieter in your life, or possibly removed. If you are serious about change, you have to consider muting someone or removing your connection to them online, or, reducing how much you see them or interact with them in real life. I fully respect how this can be difficult, but your mental well-being and success are too important to allow consistent damaging influences.

8. Go help others in need.

It's easy to get lost working on yourself and advocating for the changes you support. However, a huge part of your success with change at work (and in life) will depend on those who are not currently in the power structure. We're witnessing the beginning of a tidal wave of demographic change at work. As the older generations retire, women, minorities, and young people will be taking over in massive numbers. Your opportunity as a change maker is to be proactive with this trend. Seek to be an ally, coach, or mentor when the opportunity presents itself.

A similar thought can be shared about your personal life. When we think about issues and what matters, we often think about our parents, family, friends, people at work, people at church, etc. Understandable. These groups dominate your life. Just know that most people on the planet exist outside of your circles. Thus, actively seeking to interact with them and understand them benefits anyone and everyone interested in positive change. When you seek to be helpful, it's often amazing what the recipient of your assistance will teach you.

9. *Connect with people who can help you grow.*

Any professional, no matter what level of development they have reached, can always benefit from the guidance of someone who knows more. This might be a friend, a coach, or maybe a mentor. No matter what kind of change you're envisioning, given the amount of work and risks involved, you're wise to work with them to think through your strategy.

Who is this person in your life? You might know them. You might need to find them. You might need to hire them. Your company might have coaches on staff. Speak to your network and ask for referrals if you want to find one in the market. In either case, you should be investing time in finding a mentor, whether they are inside your firm or not. The best way to learn how to be a coach or mentor to others is to first humble yourself and be a good mentee, so you can see how it's done.

When you approach them regarding making change in your life, be careful and be thoughtful. This can be a weighty topic. You should be prepared to address more than the general issues of creativity, innovation, and change. Show up with one or two main targets identified, not just generic notions and desires. Also show up with having thought about your main options for moving forward, the pros and cons, resources needed, etc. Respect them and their time by doing a reasonable amount of homework first. When you do all of this, strive to be clear and brief, then after you share your thoughts and questions, do the most important thing – listen.

10. Eliminate unnecessary negativity.

First, what is the biggest failure or setback in your past you need to remember and study? Failure is a defining characteristic of success. Identify one or two you have tried to forget. Stop ignoring them.

Analyze them. Articulate something you can learn from them. Focus on the fact that you survived and will try, fail, and survive again on your journey. Use this difficult event as part of conversations with those in your inner circle.

Next, with a specific change goal in mind, think about the main hater or two who might stand in your way. This is an old organizational trick: plan your change, but early on identify potential resistors and figure out how to deal with them. Dealing with them might mean co-opting them by somehow convincing them to be on your team, or it might be working around them, or even no longer having a relationship with them. Ending relationships is of course a last resort, but as I've asked several times – how bad do you want this change?

Finally, the most difficult part is to think about negative people in your life irrespective of how they might relate to a particular goal you're chasing. As alluded to earlier, it might be a friend from back in the day or even a family member. Just because you love someone or once did, does not mean you must continue to invest in the relationship. If they have a strong net negative effect on your mental state, you must rethink the situation. Don't justify receiving bad vibes based only on past ties or shared blood. I recognize how personal such a statement might sound, but real success requires a serious support team and an absence of unnecessary negativity. You need a lot of positive energy. It's precious and finite, so don't let someone steal it.

Now you're ready. Good luck.

Live hard!